GW00391218

1

Benjamin Kell was born in Andover, and grew up in Emsworth, Hampshire. He studied History at the University of Plymouth, specialising in Asian History. He has travelled China extensively, and lived in Cambodia. This is his first book.

Thanks and Acknowledgments

First and foremost, I would like to thank my then partner, who not only provided me with a base in China, but also tolerated my incessant bleating about composing this collection of works. Without her assurance and assistance I would have struggled greatly.

Secondly, I would like to thank all those who took part and gave up their time, sharing their hopes and dreams with me. They responded with detail and attention to questions which many like them would have declined to answer. Their willingness and frankness have provided me with a truly unique and fascinating insight into this new generation. I am deeply grateful.

Thirdly, I would like to thank my college lecturer. Choosing to study Chinese history at the age of sixteen was the most important academic step I took, and our trip to China ignited my love affair with the Middle Kingdom. His support and interest in me since has helped me to shape and develop my thoughts further, and I think this compilation is all the better for it.

Finally, I would like to thank my university dissertation tutor, who not only encouraged me to dive deeper and further into Chinese history than perhaps I would have done, but who also guided me as I traversed oral and gender history. Without his expertise and guidance this book would never have come to fruition.

Contents

Author's Note

There are a few Chinese terms which crop up regularly throughout the interviews, which I feel should be explained a bit here.

Bai fu mei means 'white, rich and beautiful'. Fair skin has always been considered beautiful in China, as it depicts a life of luxury indoors, rather than the dark skin associated with the peasants toiling in the fields as well as the 'barbarians' to the south. The term *bai fu mei* is not only used to describe individuals who seem to have been dealt a winning hand in life, but is used in such a way as to imply that there is a new community of fair-skinned, beautiful and wealthy girls who are affecting the Chinese mind-set.

Po xie is a particularly crude term, which is rarely voiced. It means 'used shoe', and is a very vulgar way to describe a woman who has lost her virginity, the similarity being that both the woman and the shoe have been broken in and used by a man and then discarded, and are now useless, second-hand goods. For many Chinese of this new generation, this phrase epitomises the old, backward culture they are trying to throw off as they embrace the 21st century. Similar phrases include *mu gou* and *biao zi*, both of which are very offensive ways to describe women sexually active out of wedlock, or involved with several lovers.

Nu shen means goddess, and is used to describe the most desirable of women. Although many *nu shen* probably fit the criteria to be a *bai fu mei* as well, the term *nu shen* also highlights personality and character. In Shanghai, a friend and I walked past a poster of a Chinese actress, famous not only for her good looks and incredible figure but also for her intelligence and philanthropic activities. My friend paused in front of the poster, sighed with lustful wonder, and whispered '*nu shen*'.

Guan xi is a term which is becoming understood in the West, particularly amongst those who do business with Asian companies. Translated as 'relationship', it refers to how well connected an individual is, often in a professional context but also in terms of social standing. To have links within the police, government or military would be to have *guan xi*, and in traditional China these links would be the easiest way to a comfortable, well paid job. Although recent crack-downs on corruption have largely replaced the need for *guan xi* with academic merit, the notion of courting officials and businessmen is still common, and is tied in with the notion of 'giving face'.

Xiao bai lian means to have a 'little white face', and is used to describe men who are subservient to their wives. Indeed, there are many such idioms to describe men who don't wear the trousers in their relationships, so to speak. To 'eat soft rice' or to have 'soft ears', mean similar things. In traditional China the husbands would be expected to financially support the family alone, and women were to stay at home. For a women to earn more, and to have a more dominant status in the relationship, can be considered to bring shame to the man for his inability.

Shui de qu chu po er nu de qu chu jia means that 'a daughter who is married away is like spilled water', meaning that it has lost all value; just as water spilled from a cup soaks into the ground and is wasted, a daughter that is married into another family is lost to her own. As the daughter becomes the property of another family, her parents lose her as a worker around the house or in the rice fields. The idiom also coincides with the Confucian attitudes that daughters are not worth educating; why invest in and cherish something that will be lost to another?

De si cong san is a notion so embedded in Chinese culture that no interviewee actually bothered to mention it during their interview, taking it for granted that we were both familiar with it already. It was only during an informal chat with one of them that the idiom itself came to light. *De si cong san* means 'the three [men] to be obeyed, and the four virtues'. The 'three to be obeyed' by the woman are her father before marriage, her husband after marriage, and her sons after her husband's death. At no point in her life is a woman to be free from servitude to a male. The 'four virtues' are: to follow the moral and social codes regarding how women should behave, to beautify herself for the benefit of males, to keep quiet around company in case her views causes offence or boredom, and finally to ensure the housework is done and the children are cared for. This is perhaps the most daunting cultural relic the women of New China to have to overcome.

All these terms either directly crop up in the interviews or are underlying themes, and all are explained and challenged and adapted for twenty-first century China. How the interviewees react to the idea that tradition dictates that they should stay at home and make themselves beautiful for their husbands is to see how New China is grappling with the past in order to step unimpeded into the future.

Methodology

Before detailing the methods and means I used to arrive at these interviews, I wish to make something clear; this is a primary, not a secondary source. I have not included any analysis or evaluation in this book. The interviews are transcribed, word for word as far as I can, and left (for the most part) unedited and unexplained. The relations between location, wealth, family background, education and the like are for the reader to ascertain and justify.

Background

I compiled this book in order to understand China, New China, better. I touched upon Chinese gender roles for my undergraduate dissertation, and wished to explore it further, and to understand how it has developed in the last few decades. I decided that the way to do this was to come up with a series of penetrating, insightful questions and put them to individuals sourced within the United Kingdom that I felt represented New China. Both the criteria I used for sourcing interviewees and the questions are detailed below.

Criteria

There were several criteria which deemed an individual eligible, in my mind, for my research. Firstly, gender; she had to be female. Although I am sure Chinese men would be able to give me interesting insights and details on the roles of women, it will only ever be through their eyes, and their theories and ideas about what life is like for a woman would always be removed. For that reason, only Chinese females would do.

Obviously, nationality was important. Only ethnic Chinese girls *who considered themselves Chinese* would, I felt, give me the answers I wanted. I had the option of interviewing British-born Chinese (BBCs for those in-the-know) but I thought that this would run in to obstacles; I envisaged asking about what life is like for Chinese girls and being met with a blank face and the response 'But, I'm from Leeds…' For argument's sake, I have also included interviewees from Hong Kong. Although many Hong Kong citizens feel themselves apart from China, politically speaking they are now part of the People's Republic of China. Indeed, their tumultuous history and their mixed identity has led to some very revealing interviews. Although many may disagree with their inclusion in this study, I have justified it as so; racially, culturally, linguistically (Cantonese obviously being a Chinese language) and politically, Hong Kong is now a part of China.

The third factor was age. The candidates had to be between eighteen and twenty-five. This is for the important reason that none of them can remember the events of Tiananmen Square all those years ago; they have not experienced any of the great tragedies that befell China. They have grown up in New China, post-Deng Xiaoping China. These girls I am interviewing truly represent a changing country. As they have grown older, they have become accustomed to the new technology and influences of the twenty-first century.

They have grown up with colour TVs, smart phones and Wi-Fi. They embody what China, indeed all emerging super powers, wish to be seen as; rich, educated, happy.

The final factor is a foreign education. To me, studying abroad is truly a luxury. It is not a frivolous spend or a treat; it is an investment costing thousands and thousands of pounds. It also reflects the attitude of the family; investing this time and money and effort in a daughter is a far cry from the norm just fifty or sixty years ago. To me, it epitomises New China. The focus on education, the long term investment, the pressure on the individual, the sacrifice of the family unit, all epitomise New China. These women, some of whom will graduate from Oxford or Harvard, will be the CEOs and politicians of tomorrow. Other girls (the vast, vast majority of Chinese girls) who leave school at an early age to work in retail or to help harvest rice do not, alas, represent New China, which is in the process of leaving them behind. That is not to say I feel their opinion worthless, far from it, but they will not be the ones changing China and pushing it forward; they and their culture have not changed, and it is that change which is the object of this study.

In addition, those who have studied abroad will most likely be more self-aware. The more I travel, the more time I spend in weird and wonderful places, the more I find out about myself and my identity. It is my opinion that only when you have experienced the cultures of other countries can you understand your own. Whether or not those who have been abroad longest will have the most refined and organised thoughts on these subjects is for the reader to ponder; duration of time abroad and locations of foreign destinations have been included.

Finally, the interviews were conducted in English. In this New China, which is aggressively engaging in international business, English is important; without it, world trade would be difficult. A good understanding of English shows not only education and prospects, but also an understanding of the world and that essential thirst for learning.

Sourcing the candidate

As a means of sourcing, I used the Snowball Method. I would initially interview friends and acquaintances, who would then recommend a friend or relative. This worked, for the most part, very well. I was able to enter with a relaxed attitude and an air of friendliness. Where this proved insufficient, I would resort to social media. Many British universities have Chinese Societies, and adverts were placed on the forum. I also ensured that I sourced a maximum of four candidates from each university. This ensured that I found people of different backgrounds. A woman studying at Plymouth University (famous for its Maritime Law and International Business schools) is going to have a different attitude to life and a different family to a woman studying at the University of Winchester (well-known for its Art and Graphics courses).

Questions and Answers

The questions have been specifically designed to encourage the interviewees to open up, and to relate to experiences they themselves have come across. This allows for much more depth and fluidity; it is for this reason also that I have included digressions in the transcripts, as they can be as enlightening as the answers themselves.

Personal Information, touching upon age, origin, family life and education

This may well be the most important section; it shows where they are from, where they have been, what their family does, what they have studied. It makes the interview personal, a story with a history and people and emotions. Secondly, it offers quantitative data: links between wealth, location, family background and education can be ascertained from this information.

How do you think future generations will view Chinese women in the early 21st Century?

This question attempts to uncover the differences between generations of women in China, and how it is now. A brief discussion usually preceded this answer, whilst we spoke about bound feet and Red Guards. This was a very revealing question. I was often greeted with fascinating stories regarding the lives of mothers and grandmothers. The most important thing that this reveals is the sense of self in history, and where she fits into this story of a country in transition; the interviewee is not only evaluating her life, but her position in the world, and how she, and others like her, view their places in society and history is a key insight into how they think and feel about themselves and their positions in New China.

Many young Chinese women wear clothes that would not be accepted in previous generations. Are these clothes accepted now? If so, why?

This question targeted the seemingly unrelated issue of fashion. But fashion can be a key indicator of youth culture and popular movements (anyone who has studied the punk era in British music must agree) and represents what is culturally acceptable. But questioning why it is accepted, and where these changes come from, involves further thought. The interviewee, maybe unknowingly, simply by discussing demin shorts and high heels, is giving her insight into how women portray themselves, how society views them, and how it makes them feel.

What do you think has changed most since your mother was your age? Do you think anything should change further?

This is very direct; it is asking for a reiteration of stories her mother may have passed down. What is key here is which aspects they choose to focus on to explain; some interviewees talk in depth about the fact that they can study, whilst their mother could not. Others spoke about being able to choose who to have a relationship with. This shows what is important to them as an individual. As well as directly showing what has changed, it subtly shows what factors and aspects are important in these girls' lives.

Do women have equal opportunities and rights now?

This question, again, allows for digression, elaboration, flexibility. Much like the previous question, the candidates get to explain a personal or family experience, but more importantly, they get to choose which topic to talk about. The topic they choose shows which aspects of modern life they find important and most worthy of acknowledgement.

In the UK and the US having a child out of wedlock is common. What do you think about this?

This question attempts to explore the changes in attitude between generations; the candidate gives her view on the issue, on whether it is acceptable or not. When this is explored it shows the gaps (or not) between generations. This can be a clear indicator of the values regarding marriage and family life held by New China contrasted against the expectations of Old China, and how this contrast is viewed.

Some people think that dating shows objectify and sexualise women for entertainment. What do you think? How do you think it affects the women (and men) who watch it?

Opinions on dating shows can be revealing; some find them useful tools in modern matchmaking, others find them harmless entertainment, whilst others find them crude and offensive. As with many of these questions, a sense of self and identity can be revealed through the answers. Words such as 'objectifying' and 'sexualising' are most commonly used by women who see being a woman as part of their identity. This question can also reveal the candidate's attitudes to make up and beauty, and whether they feel this is important in the new world of educated and driven women. Although the wording of the question can seem pointed, I felt it prudent to ensure that the interviewee understood what aspects of the show I was attempting to penetrate; otherwise the question could be interpreted as whether or not they simply like watching the show. It is also important to consider the fact that some of these girls may never have discussed issues such as objectifying or sexualising, certainly in English. Some explanation was needed to ensure relevant material.

When it comes to dating, what do you feel is important?

This question could be seen as strange, as it directly asks what sort of things the candidate looks for in a man (or woman). However, this is a great way to understand the values of the women of New China. The most important features a prospective husband had to have pre-Mao would have been money and influence, and during Mao's reign a strong political background. What is important now? Surely, as Chinese women become more independent and educated, money and influence in a spouse isn't as important. On the other hand, where more and more girls dress in provocative clothing and don make up, perhaps the idea of using beauty to marry into wealth is becoming a preferred route to a comfortable life.

In a relationship, what is your role? Are you equal?

Candidates are asked what their role in a relationship is, or what they think it should be. This is another question which contrasts the norms and values of old China with the expectations and hopes of the women of New China. Once they have given their answers, they are asked for the reasoning behind them. It is important to understand how these girls view themselves against men; should they unquestioningly do the housework, or should their education and skill exclude them from menial tasks?

If you could sum up Chinese attitudes to these topics in a few sentences, what would they be?

Finally, the candidates were asked to summarise how these topics would be answered by normal Chinese, or Chinese who held traditional norms and values regarding women and sex and fashion. This question again requires the interviewee to view themselves as part of a group, to have an identity. To accurately describe how middle-aged men would feel about these issues the interviewee would have to accept the differences between them and herself, and to accept that she belongs to a new group, an educated, lucky elite. It is also interesting to see how the interviewees choose to portray 'traditional culture'; it is easy to see rivalries or prejudices between different ethnic, religious or geographical groups in this section.

Layout

The composition of the interviews have been grouped by province, and listed in alphabetical order, from Beijing to Zhejiang. This is purely out of ease for research.

Anonymity

Many of the topics discussed in these interviews are very personal. For this reason, I have excluded the interviewees' real, Chinese names, and inserted in their stead English names they'd prefer to have used.

Introduction

I have always been interested in China.

I began my academic career with China and its history in college, where I was utterly gripped from the word go. I continued my studies throughout university, concluding with my dissertation, which was an examination of Mao's Red Guards and their impact upon society and traditional culture.

One of the many areas of Chinese culture that came under attack when the Red Guards were given free reign was femininity, gender roles and sex. Women were stripped of their female identity in an attempt to make them more militant; wearing skirts and sporting fashionable hairstyles became beatable offences, and women of all ages were accused of promiscuity in the most revolting language (see *po xie* in Author's Note).

There is a wealth of material available for historians studying this area. Many prolific historians and sociologists have compiled some phenomenal work, and I was able to indulge my studious side by reading for days on end. However, I began to notice a gap in the shelves, so to speak. The university library had many great books on Chinese women; from the Dragon Empress to the roles of women in the Korean War, but I couldn't find any about Chinese women now, in the twenty-first century. I decided to look online. Again, there were some fantastic books about Chinese women in the Cultural Revolution or powerful women like Jiang Qing, but very little on Chinese women now, in New

China. Considering the impact they will have on the world, and are already having, I thought this decidedly unjust. I determined to give the matter more thought.

After my dissertation had been submitted, I found life rather empty. I went back to my old job, but I couldn't stop thinking about this area of study which seemed almost empty. In the evenings I would devote myself to further research, and finally began to formulate some questions. I ploughed through articles and text books, novels and memoirs to try and gain an understanding of the world I was about to try and enter. Within a few months I was driving or catching the train to different cities, and conducting interviews with some of the most interesting and engaging people I have ever met. I hope that this compilation can be as informative and eye-opening for you as it was for me.

NEW VOICES FROM NEW CHINA

BEIJING

December, 2013. Brighton, UK.

Faye is from Beijing, and was born in June 1989. She is an only child, and both her parents work for a national oil firm. She has been in the UK for four years. She studied for two years in Beijing's Technological University, two years in Portsmouth, UK, and is now in Brighton doing her Masters. In Portsmouth she studied International Trade and Business Communications, and now she is studying International Management. She has not yet travelled further than the UK, but plans to go to France, Italy and Switzerland for Christmas 2013.

How do you think future generations will view Chinese women in the early 21st Century?

Chinese women now are nearly equal to men. Especially girls; in my generation, if you are an only child, a girl, your parents spoil you more, they take care of you more. More than boys. If you are a son, parents prefer for you to be more independent. But as a girl, parents give you more money, more gifts. [This is true] for some boys, also, but always for girls. And if you have a boyfriend, normally the boyfriend will pay more. Women have overtaken men... but some men still think women should do chores, like do the cooking or housework or things like that.

Many young Chinese women wear clothes that would not be accepted in previous generations. Are these clothes accepted now? If so, why?

It is still not very normal for girls to wear overly revealing clothes. Of course you can, but I don't think people in my parents' age group would think you should wear this. Of course you can, but not too sexy, like naked! This is because China is influenced by the fashion of foreign countries, especially America, England, Japan, Korea, these countries' fashion styles. We are influenced a lot... from magazines, TV shows, really a lot.

What do you think has changed most since your mother was your age? Do you think anything should change further?

When my mother was very young, because she had two sisters and one young brother in her family... because before, Chinese people were very poor. If a family had one egg, only the boy could eat it. But now, if the family has one daughter and one son, they can share it, share the egg. It is equal now. So this has changed. My mother could not complete higher education, as her family budget was very limited, and her family could only afford the son's education; my uncle has a college education, and she only has a high school education. She still has a good job in a big company, because in my mum's generation people were like this [not formally educated], it is common. But now you cannot. I think women have come closer to securing equality.

Do women have equal opportunities and rights now?

As I said before, in a couple, the man still thinks you should do the housework or something, and that you should not have too strong an opinion. If you have an argument, the man will want to decide the outcome, and not allow the woman to do so. In school it is pretty equal, but in the world of work it is not. For lower rung places in companies it is pretty equal, but for the top jobs like executive or supervisor, normally they would not allow a woman to take this job. They think maybe a woman will be weak, and that a man is more powerful; they can make people listen to them. It is different in Hong Kong, because it has been largely influenced by the UK, but not China, China is still very traditional. In daily life, women are treated the same, exactly equally, like in the street or on the bus.

In the UK and the US having a child out of wedlock is common. What do you think about this?

I think it is very bad for the child to be brought up in a single parent family. I think that if the man looks after the child without a wife, then he may become bored of the child and not want it. If he is ambitious, and wants to work, he will not be able to spend much time with the child. And if you want to have more fun in life, or more girlfriends, a child will be a hindrance. And for a woman raising a child alone, they must be exhausted! You need to work harder to earn more money, money for the child. And women are very sensitive, and may become very depressed and think 'Oh, my life is so

31

difficult because I have a child now'. And they think that the kid is a burden. I could never do this, no. I think it would be bad for my child. And my parents are very traditional, and other people would laugh at me. My parents would kill me!

Some people think that dating shows objectify and sexualise women for entertainment. What do you think? How do you think it affects the women (and men) who watch it?

It depends on what you think of these shows. For me, it is interesting, as you can actually learn a lot form these shows. They have psychologists there, to analyse your personality, and you can see different kinds of people. And because of these psychologists you can understand these different kinds of people, and why they think the way they do. Some people are strange, but there is a reason they are so ridiculous. Every person has their own story. When the psychologists think the contestants behave like a joke, then you know you should not behave like them. It depends how you see it. As for me, I just think I would never go on this kind of show. Because some people say things they would not normally say; if you say it on TV then people will judge you, say you are this kind of person because you said this or that, but actually you are not. Men probably just watch it to learn how to catch, how to chase, a girl.

When it comes to dating, what do you feel is important?

My type needs to have a similar wealth level as me. I don't want him to be to poor. We need to have the same value of money, and spend money on things we agree on. Like, if I wanted to have a nice meal but he thinks it is too expensive, then things would be very difficult. As for looks, appearance, just normal is fine, but not ugly. There would be a lot of pressure on me if he is not good looking and I took him home to meet my family. They would think 'Oh, why does she choose this guy?!' so, yeah. Too handsome... if it doesn't affect the personality then no problem, but sometimes good looking boys are more proud, and may chase girls. As for personality, I want a nice person; outgoing, reliable, responsible. Someone who can take responsibility for his job, the family and me. I think he would need to have the same level of education as me, or perhaps a better education, because I think if it is not as good as mine he won't be able to do very well [professionally]. He will be unconfident.

In a relationship, what is your role? Are you equal?

I need to be considerate in a relationship. If he is very tired from working or studying I should notice it, and encourage him when he struggles. I would want a job too, we would support each other, both in work. As for cooking... My boyfriend is a good cook, ha ha! He usually cooks. But sometime I cook Chinese food and he cooks Japanese or American, as he is an American born Japanese. He cooks very well, and I also cook well. So we change, we swap. I would still need to look beautiful. You need to keep yourself interesting, right? Just because you have a boyfriend, doesn't mean you can dress randomly every day. Otherwise he would get bored, I think.

If you could sum up Chinese attitudes to these topics in a few sentences, what would they be?

I think that today there are still many housewives, that is, in my generation, but most now have a higher level in the relationship than in generations past. But for my mum's age, she is a housewife and always has to listen to the husband. But now, housewives feel that they have a say and discuss matters together. Same roles, but different rights in different times. Normally, if you are a housewife, it means you must have married a rich guy. So these 'housewives' are not real housewives. They will hire other people to do the cleaning for them or cooking for them and just watch TV all day; they have nothing else to do. In China, it is important for girls to get an education. But if you have a PhD, you may find it difficult to find a husband. If you are too well educated, you may scare men away.

FUJIAN

January, 2014. Winchester, UK.

Born in August 1990, Celia is from Fujian Province, Fuan city. She studied in Xiamen before coming to the UK, and she currently studies Fashion Design in Winchester. She has been in the UK for six months at the time of the interview. Before coming to the UK she went to Dubai on a holiday cruise, and has since travelled around the UK. Both her parents own their own businesses, dealing in construction. She has a younger sister and a younger brother; nineteen and eighteen respectively. Both will go to university soon, 'hopefully in Canada'.

How do you think future generations will view Chinese women in the early 21st Century?

Now, in China, people have moved on from old society and old values. There is equality between males and females. In society, in the workplace, in the street. But I cannot vouch for small communities in the country. Old attitudes can exist there. There is a city near to me, called Futian, where men still feel they are worth more than women. There, still, women cannot work, and must stay at home and take care of their children. They take care of the house and their family. They must always obey their husbands. This exists in China, not far from my hometown. I think we are equal; my parents spent, and are still spending, a lot of money to give me a good education. This is why I need to work, not just my husband, so things are equal. I think a lot of Chinese girls today think the same things as me, and value their education.

Many young Chinese women wear clothes that would not be accepted in previous generations. Are these clothes accepted now? If so, why?

They are common. I think people think differently now compared to then. Maybe they thought that women who reveal their skin and are sexy are bad, and that this should be saved for their husband. This is the rule. Sexy things should be worn in private. In public, people would think she is a prostitute. But nowadays, if a girl wears sexy clothes outside, I think it is not so bad. In the summer, in Xiamen, it is very hot. You must wear short shorts or small tops. I feel comfortable, it is ok. Opinions have changed; in olden China we were not allowed to know about other cultures. China was closed, and had no foreign influences influencing it. China had its own clothes. A lot of women wore these styles of clothes, old Chinese dresses, and other women would like them and feel they are fashionable, and copy them. But now, we can wear other things. We have changed our minds. It is just fashion, I think. My mother would wear these clothes, she likes short dresses, above the knee, but my grandmother totally disagrees. She told me she has never worn a dress, always trousers. I don't know why there is this difference between them.

What do you think has changed most since your mother was your age? Do you think anything should change further?

Maybe the change between my mother's time and my time is not very big. Because in my mother's age, in her youth, she also could have a job and be independent. It is my grandmother who was not allowed to do these things. I think in my mother's age they already had permission to do more. My mum didn't go to university though. To get into university you needed to have good grades, and a lot of money. So my mum only finished high school, and left education then to start working.

Do women have equal opportunities and rights now?

I think women have obtained equality now. When a woman is young, up to about thirty, they have children and family. But if you want to have a good job after this, there is not much opportunity. It will be hard to find a job once you have a husband and a family. Bosses might feel these women will not commit to the work, and they will not be hard working. They need to take care of their children. Maybe they wouldn't hire these women because of this. This is unequal. Because men also have a family and children, but they do not suffer. I think attitudes to women in education have changed a lot since ancient times. For example, attitudes in a rich family and a poor family are totally different. The rich people have enough money and will provide an equal education for both their son and daughter. But in a poor family, they do not. They focus on the boy. Because the boy can continue the family name. When the girl grows up, she will marry into another family. But in big cities they don't think this. Because if you have a son, you have to buy a house and, you know, in China, a house is very expensive in the cities. He would have to maybe be a doctor. So these people may prefer a daughter! Then they wouldn't have to buy a house.

In the UK and the US having a child out of wedlock is common. What do you think about this?

I can't say whether single parent families are a good thing or a bad thing. Because, in the UK, you can provide enough to have a family. But in China there are too many people. If the woman has not gotten married, and has children, maybe she will not have the time to take care of her children. But the government do not have enough money to help every Chinese person, there are too many of us! It is different for each country. It isn't acceptable in China. If I had a baby but no family, what would my parents say!? Also, it depends on the family. If you are rich, it is ok. But if you are poor, it may be a terrible thing. Because single parents cannot afford to pay for the children on their own. It takes two people, working together.

Some people think that dating shows objectify and sexualise women for entertainment. What do you think? How do you think it affects the women (and men) who watch it?

I think these dating shows are just entertainment, just for fun. I have heard a lot of reports that these girls on these shows may choose the boy, but after the show they do not get together; it doesn't really happen, it is just a show. Boys watch it to see the interaction between the man and woman, just like in a film. The girls on the show always enquire about family, education, income. Maybe boys will focus on this... but not all girls focus on this. This kind of show it is an opportunity for the boy and girl to show what they have. It doesn't really reflect boys or girls in China. The girls on this programme do this to be famous; they say these things to the world to become famous, they don't represent all Chinese girls.

When it comes to dating, what do you feel is important?

I think a potential boyfriend should have a good education, and have a good personality. Maybe, what I like is a gentleman. He must know about many things, not just luxury brands. We must be able to talk about many things. It is hard to say about wealth... if the boy works very hard and doesn't have a rich family it is ok. If he has a rich family but doesn't work hard, but goes shopping or travelling, then he isn't very good. He'll need to be a hard worker. I would like him to be close, geographically; if we worked in different countries or different cities and we couldn't meet often it would be like being single! My grandmother and grandfather never met before they married... things have changed so much.

In a relationship, what is your role? Are you equal?

I would want to be equal, of course equal! I would need to be hardworking too. If you want a good future, you have to work too! I would also want my own income, my own job. I won't want to depend on my husband. I think housework would be half-and-half too. I lived with my boyfriend in university in China. He was a Chinese too. We are still together! We have been together about five years… my father isn't happy that I lived with him, he's never happy about boys! My father has only met him once, ha ha! We rented a flat together. We met at university, through a mutual friend. I don't think we will marry, certainly not now, as my parents wouldn't tolerate it. I would have to finish my education first.

If you could sum up Chinese attitudes to these topics in a few sentences, what would they be?

I think most Chinese will have a similar view to me, except in the countryside. In Sichuan province the women's positions are higher than the men's! In the south of my province, in a city called Futian, the women always need to obey their husbands. Just like Japanese girls. They always need to work in the house and obey their husbands. They have seen few changes since the olden times, but women's positions have raised slightly. A funny thing; the family only marry their daughters to local boys, also from Futian. They will not mix with people from other cities or towns.

September 2013, Plymouth, UK.

Cara was born in February 1990. She was born in Chengdu, although moved soon after to Xiamen, and now has a Fujian residency permit. She has been in the UK one year at the time of the interview. She has been to the UK before, as well as several other European countries including France, Belgium and Holland, whilst on a European road trip with her sister's class when she was fifteen. She has four siblings; two brothers and two sisters, one younger and one older of each. Her parents deal in electrical components for businesses and construction. Her older sister studies in Canada, her younger sister is studying in China and both her brothers work for the family business. She studied Hospitality Management for her undergraduate and now studies Business Management for her Masters. This accounts for three years of university in China, and two in the UK. She studied in Beijing Normal University.

My sister had a boy chase her, a Canadian boy. She has a boyfriend now, but this was before him... he was thirty-one. She told my mum about it and she was acting like she was ok with it in front of everyone, in front of the family, and then afterwards she dragged my sister aside and told her 'No, I don't want you to have a relationship with other people'. That is what parents do.

How do you think future generations will view Chinese women in the early 21st Century?

41

I think it is getting better for women now. Before now, before 1949, women had no power to choose who they married. People now don't really listen to their parents; if your parents told you to marry this guy, you couldn't really say no, but now you can. Women have got more power. I want to find a good job, have a better life. I want to be able to decide for myself, not rely on my parents... I don't really want to do that, or rely on my husband. I want my own money, so I can spend my money on whatever I want. I could go travel and not have to ask for money from my husband. I don't think this view is so common, because Chinese girls' parents want us to marry into a family which is equal to ours, so our husbands would give us enough money to live on and we would not have to work too hard.

Many young Chinese women wear clothes that would not be accepted in previous generations. Are these clothes accepted now? If so, why?

It depends... when girls wear something like that to visit their grandparents, they will be judged. But at home, it doesn't really matter. Sometimes my mother may mention something to my sister, old fashioned views. But it's the way my sister wants to dress and the way she wants to be, and my mother can't change much. Friends don't mind so much. Young girls think that fashion is pretty, and don't really mind about it. It is just the way they want to be. I think this is due to education. We learn a lot more about everything. I mean, my grandparents didn't study; they don't have this level of education. She studied different thoughts to us, and now she's too old to study new things. She had a different education, I think this is why. I think that right now Chinese people like to learn things, to accept things form outside of China. This is why we readily accept these fashions.

What do you think has changed most since your mother was your age? Do you think anything should change further?

My mother doesn't really talk about how life was for her… she mentions that she was not wealthy, and had to spend time farming in the countryside; she had to carry a lot of stuff, and do lots of heavy work. So now, when I or my siblings are carrying something that isn't really very heavy and complain, she would say 'When we were young, when we were your age, we had to carry things a lot heavier than that!' but sometimes it just isn't comparable. Right now, we have a very different lifestyle compared to then. Back then they just had to do this stuff. They didn't have a choice.

Do women have equal opportunities and rights now?

Equality depends. It depends on where you mean. In education, I think it is equal. Girls in school are treated the same as boys, and get the same respect. In the workplace… I think it is equal too. But it depends on what work you are doing. Unequal places to work would be in construction, manufacturing. You need to be a man to do that, as we don't have as much muscle as men. But teaching, and skilled work, I think women get good opportunities and good money. But I don't work, so I don't know.

In the UK and the US having a child out of wedlock is common. What do you think about this?

It is not necessary to have a husband. If the father leaves, then the mother can find another man to help look after the baby. And if they want to do it alone... then it is their choice. If it was me, my mum would kill me! My parents would be so angry! They just don't think we should have a baby before being married, and that we should look after the baby properly. They would want me to get married around this age, twenty-three, but when I was twenty-one my mother told me there was another girl my age who was working and living in the countryside and she already had a baby, and had gotten married. That is how life in the countryside is. Where they live it is normal; you turn twenty-one, get married and have a baby. I think the reason I am not pressured into finding a husband is because I am studying; when I was going to university my mother wouldn't allow me to get a boyfriend, as it would distract me. But this is the best time to find one! Find one whilst studying, and then get married after studies. Out of my cousins, of which there are four, two are already married and have kids and one will get married in October. They are around twenty-four or twenty-five. One of their wives is only twenty-two and already has kids. In China the financial aspect is very different; parents don't care if you can afford to have a baby, they just want you to have a baby and they will look after it. They just want a grandchild! My cousin is working, and his wife looks after the children, and often leaves one with her parents, and deals with just one at a time. Because the first is a girl they tried for another, to get a boy. Before the second birth they have a test to check whether it is boy or girl. This is illegal, though. And if it were to be a girl they would have aborted it. Because in China it is not allowed to have two children. When it is found out you are often dragged away to have it aborted, no matter how old the baby is. She was able to have two because when she had the first she was living in Xiamen and five months after the birth she moved to Beijing to have the other, and nobody knew. The thing is, if you are found to be pregnant with a second baby it is aborted, but you can pay a fine if the baby has already been born; they can't just kill a baby! Horrible... if some families discovered their baby was a girl they would kill it, or just throw it in the rubbish. But I think now there is a policy in the making to allow a second baby, but I don't know when that will be announced.

Some people think that dating shows objectify and sexualise women for entertainment. What do you think? How do you think it affects the women (and men) who watch it?

These dating shows are terrible... I think it is just entertainment, just a show. I have heard someone say that these girls are chosen and they are actors. And the guys just go up and make things up. All the things in the show are made to happen, it is just entertainment, and I don't like it. It is just too fake. I don't think it degrades women; if you want to go, you can go. If you don't, you don't. It is up to the individual woman. But for men, sometimes I think it makes them feel insecure as all the men on the show say they are rich and clever. These women just want money, that's all they want. People at home like us just see it as fun, as entertainment, we don't really care about it. But people where I'm from don't really watch this stuff. I definitely don't watch it, and my sisters don't watch it. But sometimes, maybe my mum and dad watch it. It is often watched by older people I think.

When it comes to dating, what do you feel is important?

For me, I think that emotional connections and personality are important. It is important to connect with someone's emotions if you are close to them. And if they are really, really, really ugly, extremely ugly, then that isn't good, ha ha! Education isn't so important, as long as we have something in common and we can talk. Money isn't important, I don't really care. If we really want to be together we'll just have to work hard and earn money for ourselves. That's what I think. So he has to be a hard worker! My parents would want me to be in love! They would also want wealth, and education, good academic or political connections, close location… everything! They would want me to find a boy who is on the same level as our family. Because our parents just want us to have a good life, they don't want us to work hard like they did at our age because it was really hard, they want us to skip that part and enjoy our lives.

In a relationship, what is your role? Are you equal?

I think we should be equal in a relationship; if I was to cook, he is to clean the dishes, that's what I want. I want it equal. I really hate it when my mum asked me to clean the dishes because every time we have a meal together; we finish our food and my mum tells me to clean the dishes, and she doesn't ask my brothers. I hate it so much! This is partly because I'm a girl. Sometimes she doesn't even ask my older sister, just me, and I really, really hate it. I hate cleaning the dishes, I want it to be equal and share the responsibility with my siblings. Anyway, financially, he can earn his money and I can earn my money. And when we go out, he pays for me sometimes and I pay for him sometimes. I don't think it matters who earns more, but I think to some men it matters. Some think they should earn more than women, as it makes them manlier. But I don't care.

If you could sum up Chinese attitudes to these topics in a few sentences, what would they be?

I think right now Chinese culture is still diverse, mainly due to location. In the south they tend to be more old-fashioned and people in the north, like Beijing and Shanghai and Manchuria, are more modern. In my province, Fujian, they are really old fashioned, like what I have said about my parents. But I don't know that much about other places. Because people in China, when they are young, when they are in primary school or high school, they will stay in one place; most will then move to other provinces for university. But some find an agreeable place, and stay in the same place. Chinese don't tend to travel alone, certainly not until after college, and often only for education.

GUANGDONG

August, 2013. Near Portsmouth, UK

Edith is from Shenzhen, a large city on the coast of Guangdong which looks out towards Hong Kong. She is a student, having spent one year in Guangzhou University and two at Plymouth University in the UK. She is now on a placement work year and lives close to Portsmouth, Hampshire, with her British boyfriend and his family.

Her mother is from Qinghai province, and her father is from Gansu province. She was born in Gansu, in May 1991. She spent her childhood in her hometown, and then she and her family moved to Shenzhen when she was nine years old. Both her parents worked for the government as engineers until they moved to Shenzhen, where they settled down. Both her parents now work for private companies as engineers.

How do you think future generations will view Chinese women in the early 21st Century?

I think women are more equal now than in the past. You can't have more than one wife now, and the law protects the woman. You get more female rights, that sort of thing, you get protected. Also, the society… let's say you are married and you have relationship or sex with another woman, your friends and the whole society will think you're a bad man, and I think that's the whole of society respecting women more. They have more financial and political rights too. At my age, in a relationship, the boy will think he needs to do more, and the girl tends to be bossy. At a young age, even before a proper job and before finishing education, girls will think 'Oh, the boys should buy me dinner, buy me clothes, treat me well', and the boys think they should do the same thing, that they should do as the girls think. But after they are married the girl will think 'I have to do the housework, I have to make my husband comfortable, I have to make him dinner, take care of the kids.' So when they are married the woman will take more responsibility in the house. I think before marriage they expect the man to treat them well. Not just bags or make up, but the man should do more to protect them and care for them. But after they get married, I think the husband will take a more controlling role. Women step down from being in control.

Many young Chinese women wear clothes that would not be accepted in previous generations. Are these clothes accepted now? If so, why?

Girls tend to wear lots of short shorts, but you hardly see any girls in China wearing low cut tops... yeah, I think that's true. People don't think wearing short shorts is sexual. They think 'It's not weird, it's hot!' But normal girls, good girls, not slutty ones, don't wear low cut strap tops or tops which reveal figures, but certainly the short shorts are accepted. I think it's because China is more open, more Westernised. Lots of Western-designed clothes are now available in China. We go 'Oh, that looks good.' Or maybe Western values are just coming out without us realising. Yeah, maybe it's that. I don't know, people just wear them. Like dresses... when my mum was young, in the early eighties, they didn't have short shorts, but they had dresses down to the knee. Then in the 90s... people were still caring about exposing their body. I think this generation people definitely wear less clothes.

What do you think has changed most since your mother was your age? Do you think anything should change further?

For most women of my mum's generation, their family wouldn't let them travel alone or meet up with boys. She told me when they were under eighteen, meeting a boy on their own was considered really, really bad. It was fine to go as a group, but if my mum went out with a boy, just the two of them, and their family friends were to see them, they would tell her parents 'Your girl is going out with a boy, on the street' and things like that. That's definitely changed. We can make more choices. But there is still an age limit; you have to be a certain age. My mum's generation, all my mum's friends I know, they wouldn't let their kids, until maybe after university, have a proper boyfriend or girlfriend. At least until they finish high school, around eighteen. But two of my mum's friends, couples I know, are *really* uptight about their daughters. They don't want their daughters to have boyfriends, or get close to a boy, so their daughter won't mention boys in front of her parents. She still talks to boys, and talks about boys, but she can't say anything in front of her parents. So the level of this change depends on the particular family. I think when people of my generation become parents, we will be more open up about relationships. We won't say 'You are too young to meet up with boys until you are eighteen'. Because my mum's generation still thinks that studies should come first. They think if a girl has a boyfriend at sixteen she will mess up her studies, or the boy may try and have sex with her. My friend's mum is quite open, but not her dad. My friend won't tell her dad, even now, she has a boyfriend. I don't know when the age for my mum's generation is. What will change is that our generation will be more open about relationships. But I wouldn't be happy knowing my children go around having sex, or go to a club. I don't want my future daughter to meet up with boys and sleep around.

Do women have equal opportunities and rights now?

It depends on where you go as to how women are treated. In big cities, in rich parts, women are probably equal with men in employment terms. Women can also get promoted; they will not bar you because you are a woman. If you can get into a company, that is enough. In China, like many countries, women tend to work as secretaries or bar girls whilst the manager is a man. But I think it is more about skills. Maybe in some respects women aren't as suited [to professional work] as men. Women have to take time off for maternity leave, and because of this men put in more effort at work. Maybe

51

I'm influenced by society's view that 'men are better'. I think that is still the way in China. When I think of a doctor or professor or scientist I automatically think of a male. If a man who is married stays at home to look after the kids and cooks and the woman goes out to work then people will think he is soft. Men shouldn't rely on women. They would say he 'eats soft rice' *chi wan fan* or *xiao bai lian* which means he has a 'little white face'. But it's fine for a woman to stay at home all day, take care of the kids, and not have a job. I don't want to marry a man who is happy to stay at home and look after the kids, I think that is inefficient. But I don't want a husband who tells me not to work, to stay at home and look after kids. I think equality is needed.

In the UK and the US having a child out of wedlock is common. What do you think about this?

I think single parent families are sad. I think it shows the man is horrible for leaving the woman and the baby. If the baby was an accident, why did they decide to keep the baby but not commit to each other? If the woman wants to do it alone, that's fine, but she should look for another husband. Even if her future husband doesn't mind she had a kid already with another man, I think the man's family, particularly the mum, wouldn't approve. To have a baby in marriage and then divorce is ok, because it shows you were in a proper relationship, committed, and no one will say 'You are a used shoe, why do you have a baby around?' people would just say 'You are divorced.' The mother of the new boy would say to him 'If you are happy with the baby, and to be a stepfather, that's fine.' But if you are not married and you have a child, and then you want another family to accept you, you will run into difficulty. Chinese people will think you irresponsible, or will sleep around, and are unable to commit. They think it shows a lack of caring. Although this isn't the truth, people will think her life is messy, and that she is not a good woman.

Some people think that dating shows objectify and sexualise women for entertainment. What do you think? How do you think it affects the women (and men) who watch it?

I think dating shows are just shows, definitely not real, just an entertainment show… but definitely influenced by notions of being beautiful and having the women all looking the same. Women on the show are encouraged to look the same. To attract a wider audience to watch, they get attractive women to go the stage. What they want to show the audience are women who adhere to the ideas of beauty. I think both men and women share the control on these shows. The male contestant can choose to an extent, but women have the final say and can back out when they choose… which means women are in control, in general. To an extent it empowers women; they are given their beauty and talent and wealth and are allowed to choose what they do and which man to date. They are rich, pale and beautiful. So they are considered the peak of beauty. We call them *bai fu mei;* 'white, rich, beautiful'. They are considered 'goddesses', *nu shen.* All the boys chase them. So on these dating shows all the girls all have good jobs, are beautiful and are pale, even though it is just make up. And the host will focus on these points and point them out to the man, as a bit of a joke. It points out the superficial things rather than the individual traits. I do think they view women as items. I feel weird seeing lots of girls lined up and a man choosing one; they are viewed as items. I think this attitude can encourage men to view women as less. All the men watching the show can say 'Oh, I can choose these women too' and play along at home. They play along at home, and speak with their friends about the best or ugliest women. And the girls who watch this show will watch and think 'I wish I could get a man like that'. I think it makes men think they are better, but they are encouraged to try and impress the women. They always focus on their fitness and their wealth and their family rather than personal qualities.

When it comes to dating, what do you feel is important?

I do judge people by their looks. I don't care if they are not good looking, but I wouldn't want to be their girlfriend, just friend. Just mediocre looking I don't mind. If I saw a handsome boy I wouldn't think 'He is so handsome, I will chase him', I wouldn't do that. A caring attitude towards others is important, as is his honesty and reliability and truthfulness. Money would come in the next stage of the relationship. When dating money doesn't matter, but when I'm planning to get married... I don't want to live in a shed. I don't care about family connections so much. If I had been dating a boy for three or four years and want to get married, I wouldn't marry him until we have saved up enough to rent a flat and live comfortably. I wouldn't rush into it. But I wouldn't marry a boy who is too rich either! It would be scary, he may be nice but his family will be really materialistic. I think really rich people must be materialistic and chase money. They may not show it but they won't want to eat rubbish food or drive rubbish cars. Everyone has their own standards, which again is why I can't marry a very poor boy.

In a relationship, what is your role? Are you equal?

As a girlfriend, I wouldn't mind what our roles would be; I just don't like being told what to do. I definitely don't want him to stay at home all day or play around all day. Even if I earned a lot I wouldn't want him to stay at home, people would think he is soft. I don't want a lazy man. I would probably want him to earn the same as me, or a bit more. Not too much more, or he will assume control and think his money is a source of power. He might tell me what to do, and I wouldn't want that.

If you could sum up Chinese attitudes to these topics in a few sentences, what would they be?

I think it is hard to give a Chinese cultural perspective on this; it depends where in China you mean. China is very big. In the south women tend to be more controlling. I think marriage is a line in the sand, if you see what I mean. Before marriage, the ball is in the girl's court. She can choose which boy to have and demand

55

good treatment. But after marriage the man is in control. He buys her stuff and placates her, but he is really in control. Originally, people in the south much more traditional than those in the north… girls are worth less than men etc. Manchurians and people from the north-east are more relaxed. In the south families will keep having babies until they have a son, but in the north they don't care so much if they just have a daughter. Where my mum was born people don't really care that much, even peasants. People do want to have a boy but people from the south are more concerned with it. Even now, in poorer areas, girls are viewed as worth much, much less [than boys]. During high school I went to Jiangxi and stayed with a family which had a boy and two daughters. The boy could cycle to school, the girls had to walk. The boy could eat at the table, the girls had to eat on their own. We had to drag the girls to the table to eat together. The boy never cleaned, always the girls. In the city it is different, more equal. Maybe even the other way around, as boys have to work harder to impress their family and girlfriend.

GUIZHOU

September, 2013. Plymouth, UK

Summer was born in May 1992 in Guizhou province, which is in the south-west of China. She moved to Sichuan after graduating middle school, and continued her studies in Chengdu, the capital city of Sichuan. She moved there for her parent's work; they work as hydroelectric engineers, utilising Sichuan's vast number of rivers and waterways. They are both from Guizhou, and met in school as classmates. Summer has been in the UK for two and a half years; she studies Business Administration for her Masters. She has been to Hong Kong and Korea as well as the UK.

How do you think future generations will view Chinese women in the early 21st Century?

Right now, China has become more open, as so many children go abroad and study the culture from other countries. They have become more open, this generation. Their minds change, following the Western countries. But for the last generation, the generation of my grandparents, they are always traditional. Women are freer now in China. They are more equal, freer. Some women are stronger than their men! It is hard to say, it is easiest to divide into areas I think. So, if a girl was to find a job, better than her husband, she will be stronger. Even traditional women have changed. Maybe now some husbands stay at home to look after the baby and the woman goes out to earn money. Not too many, as in China men are supposed to be stronger than women. When most women get married they stay at home and take care of the babies and the household. It's hard to say what drives Chinese women. For me, I just want to find a good job if I graduate. If I am lucky, I can find a job in the UK. I know that recently it has been hard to find a job in the UK… maybe I would go back, but I'd like to stay. The life here is nice, and the weather here is cooler, and, well, I just like the life here. It is more convenient than China, and lots less people! But for some girls at university in China, they want to find a boy, a man, who is rich because maybe in the future they don't want to have to work and they want to buy luxuries. Some girls are still like this, but we are wiser now, cleverer. They want to find a good job and work for themselves, not to rely on their man. That is, if they are strong enough.

Many young Chinese women wear clothes that would not be accepted in previous generations. Are these clothes accepted now? If so, why?

I think it is ok to wear these new, revealing styles of clothing, why not? It's too hot in China! If you wear less, it is cooler. Some accept these, for some it's ok. Before this, maybe during the seventies or eighties, women always wore dresses, not small or revealing tops and shorts. At this time China was too closed. Before Deng Xiao Ping, China was always closed, and changed on its own, without the influences of others. But Deng

Xiao Ping opened up, and more Chinese can now go out. I think this is why it is more accepted now.

What do you think has changed most since your mother was your age? Do you think anything should change further?

Before I went to university my mother didn't allow me to go out after dinner. At this time I was in high school or middle school, and studying was the most important thing for me, for students... study, study, study, with no time to play or rest. But after university, when I go back for the summer holidays, I always meet my high school friends and go and eat with them or go to karaoke. Not too late, maybe ten o'clock or eleven o'clock, and my mum even allows me to drink alcohol (I don't like it, so I don't drink it). So the difference is that when my mum was young there was no karaoke! I think that boys are allowed to play later than girls. In China, most parents thinks girls should not stay out very late because they are girls, but for boys they say 'It's ok, you can stay out late. You want to come back tomorrow? That's fine'. It is hard to say if this will change... China has a strong culture, and most are quite traditional. From the old generation, traditional thinking is passed down to their children. Traditional minds... I don't think this will change soon. Not too fast, but maybe it will change in the future. But not now.

Do women have equal opportunities and rights now?

It's hard to say if women are treated equally. In China, most companies are looking for boys rather than girls. They think boys are more capable, and girls are weaker. They can't carry as much. Some jobs... it depends. But in education I think it's equal. In the northern areas of China or in villages or the countryside they think boys are more important than girls. I think it can depend on the family.

In the UK and the US having a child out of wedlock is common. What do you think about this?

I think for most Chinese girls love is the most important thing, and then get married, and then have sex... or love, then sex, then marry. Because love is important, their feelings are important. But I think in the West, for Western girls, it is more like sex, marriage, love, or sex, love, marry. It is different. I think the biggest difference is that Western women have a more relaxed culture. There is more openness in the West. Love is most important to Chinese girls. I think love and marriage is important. I'd want to find 'Mr Right' before getting married or having babies. I would never have a baby outside of marriage. I have a traditional mind; my mum brought me up like that. If I had a baby out of wedlock they would go crazy, angry! They'd be very angry at me! Girls need to be chaste before marriage, before love.

Some people think that dating shows objectify and sexualise women for entertainment. What do you think? How do you think it affects the women (and men) who watch it?

I think those dating shows are just entertainment… most of the gossip which takes place after the show says that the couples break up. They break up straight away; it's all a show, just entertainment. It's all a bit of a joke, not love. It doesn't really devalue anything, it's just a show. It's for my spare time, to waste time.

When it comes to dating, what do you feel is important?

If I hadn't communicated with a boy, and didn't know what he was like in his day to day life… for me, I would need to consider all things. How he treats girls in his daily life is important. If I didn't know his life before me, then I would need to get to know him, become friends first. A potential boy would need wisdom, to be clever. A smart person, and also intelligent. And their family education must be ok. Their family must be open minded, because family relations must be good. I must be able to have a good relationship with the boy's family, particularly his mother. That is also important, and that his family is kind. Money isn't so important, as long as he works hard and has an aim. If he is rich enough to have no aim, we wouldn't suit. Maybe one day, if he relies on his family's money, it will run out, and when there is no money left the future will be hard! If he has no aim we would have a difficult future. As long as he is not too ugly then it will be fine, ha ha! Or just normal, but not too handsome or otherwise he would be hard to handle, ha ha! Also, no less than 175cm tall. Although I am small, sometimes I may wish to wear high heels… just not too tall.

In a relationship, what is your role? Are you equal?

I think when I get a boyfriend I must work. I want to find a job, because if you stay at home it is hard to get to know new people, you'll have fewer friends. Many old friends will work and every day you will stay at home and get bored. So if I get a boyfriend or get married I must work too. Different people have different opinions, so I can accept that some would wish to stay at home because they just want an easy job, with not much pressure, and yet have a nice life without being tired every day. I think equality is important; I need to be respected too.

If you could sum up Chinese attitudes to these topics in a few sentences, what would they be?

I think most Chinese people would agree with my views on these things. Those people who have a good education would think so. Their wives too will have a good education. But if they were born in a village, in the countryside, and didn't study in primary school, they wouldn't agree with me. They would just want to have a nice wife and lots of babies. This is their outlook on life. They wouldn't want their women to go to school or work, just look after the baby and the household.

HEBEI

January, 2014. Portsmouth, UK.

Laura was born in November 1991 in Shijiazhuang city, Hebei province. Her father is a businessman, and her mother is an accountant. She finished her compulsory education in her hometown, and proceeded to do her degree in Beijing Central University of Finance and Economics. She is now studying at the University of Portsmouth, studying International Trade and Business Communication. This is her first time to go abroad. She has a small family; her mum, her dad and herself, a 'typical family' in China. She is 'crazy' about reading novels and listening to music. Since high school, she has read novels every day, including a variety of themes such as romance, war and history. In her free time she listens to English music, despite the language barrier which can be 'difficult when listening to singing'. If she has any time left after this, she does her studying.

How do you think future generations will view Chinese women in the early 21st Century?

I think every woman has a different experience of life, both now and before, but things have changed a lot. I believe that women are equal now, we have equal shares in things, and nowadays, as people have become more and more headstrong and determined, few people like the girl who adheres to traditional values, like girls who sit alone, and spend most of their time at home. Many women fight for equal rights, fight for more rights, and have obtained the rights we have now, but we need to think deeper than that; we lost good things too. According to research, the rate of divorce in China is becoming increasingly high, almost the same as the rate of marriage! The most common reason is actually that the man cannot stand having a woman whose achievements are more than his. When couples divorce or break up, the reason given by the man is always 'You are very good in all aspects, very well educated, and I do not deserve you.' The woman's virtues are the reasons for the break up! Some people say the real reason is that the man is poorer, that the woman has her own fortune, and that the man feels insecure. But the reason given is always that she is too virtuous. All these divorces and break ups show that some things were better before. Also, women have lost their traditional virtues. For example, the simplest one; nowadays, women can hardly cook! What's more they never go in the kitchen, maybe they don't know the appearance of onions, ginger or garlic! Some of them will say 'We have money, we don't need to cook for ourselves'. However, when the family comes home after a hard day at work or school, who would not want to have a warm meal was waiting for them? The meal may not be good looking as in the restaurants, but it represents the home, the family, the haven, safety. Sorry, I have gone off topic! I am not sure historians will view modern Chinese women in the future, but I think the rate of divorce will continue to grow. Maybe there will be more strong women, women with doctorates or female scientists. I think people will become more mean, more uncaring. I am not sure what this world will be like, in the future.

Many young Chinese women wear clothes that would not be accepted in previous generations. Are these clothes accepted now? If so, why?

This tends to be at home, you know? They wear normal clothes out the house, when they go out, but wear shorts and things around the house, where no one can see them. It is interesting that we can buy these things, I think it shows a big break away from feudal society, ancient thought, you know? Of course, now some girls even wear such clothes out of the house, in the street! I don't, I don't like to show too much skin, but many girls like to dress this way. I think that, since Deng Xiao Ping, we have opened up and been influenced by foreign cultures. But this only accounts for the fashion, not the mindset that allows us to accept it. I don't know why we have changed the way we think.

What do you think has changed most since your mother was your age? Do you think anything should change further?

I think it is society or the government policies which have changed the most… it is amazing that just one or two people can change the whole direction of society! Women back then didn't receive equal treatment as men. Many women were not educated, as their families preferred for the boy to go to school. I mean, I know so many Chinese girls who study here, just in Portsmouth.

Imagine how many there are in the UK, or the US! This could never have happened in my mother's time, it just couldn't. I think society's ethics, and morality, need to significantly improve; if people don't know how to be a good woman or man, what is right or wrong, it doesn't matter whether they have more money or better degree. People need to treat each other better. Not just man and woman, you know, but rich and poor and people from different areas.

Do women have equal opportunities and rights now?

Yes, I feel that we now have equal opportunities. They have equal opportunities at work, at home, at school or on the street; they have equal status. Everywhere things are getting better. You know, at school, teachers prefer girls. It is true! They used to prefer boys, but now they prefer girls. Girls are better behaved, and sometimes boys like to smoke or go and eat rather than study hard. Girls always get better grades. And at home my father often does the cooking. This is common, many fathers cook. Because both of my parents work, why should only one, the woman, do all the housework? This is normal now.

In the UK and the US having a child out of wedlock is common. What do you think about this?

Actually I don't understand what the meaning of "out of wedlock" is; is that where the child has no formal proof of birth? [I explained the meaning] Ah, I see. It is a 'black household'. In Chinese the phrase is 'illegitimate child'. The child would be bullied by other children. They will laugh at him, look down him and bully him until he is strong enough to fight for himself. I think it is a bad thing. Under these circumstances, the child may be stronger than others, may be more self-reliant, but their mental health will be damaged or distorted. They will be self-abased for no reason; perhaps they will hide this inside themselves, but it is still there.

Some people think that dating shows objectify and sexualise women for entertainment. What do you think? How do you think it affects the women (and men) who watch it?

Now women place less emphasis on dating or marriage, which I think leads to the high rate of divorce, which is getting higher. I think some modern women are lacking self-respect, and cannot morally compare with the previous 'traditional' girl at all. I think they don't respect themselves or the value of dating or marriage, and they never learn how to get others to respect them. These shows are just about face value, just about the face, or the body, and this is so stupid. If the relationship starts like this, imagine how it will end! So quickly! If people watch these shows and think like this when they find a partner, I think it will cause many problems in the future.

When it comes to dating, what do you feel is important?

When it comes to dating, I still believe that the most important thing is to find a matching soul, a soul mate.

Interests and feelings are the most important things which I value. I think in the old Chinese saying, Chinese traditional marriage ceremonies pay attention to being the perfect match; the couple will have the same status, because this means that they have the same background, same education, and they will have a common language, similar value or worldview.

In a relationship, what is your role? Are you equal?

Equality is the prerequisite. However, regardless of what it is like at home, when we are outside, it is essential to give the man enough obedience to support his face, because his face is also my face. Do you know what I mean? In China we have this concept of 'face', which means I must respect him and be compliant. If I argue with him or look down on him whilst outside, he will look like a bad boyfriend, and I will look like a poor girlfriend! I still believe love or marriage without bread is certainly not a happy one, but I pay more attention a person's character, morality. As I said earlier, if someone have no ethics but he has more money or a degree, he is just a rich animal.

If you could sum up Chinese attitudes to these topics in a few sentences, what would they be?

Chinese culture is profound, and its academic records are extensive. We are still influenced by ancient events. Do you know the Warring States period? This happened over 2000 years ago, and yet we are still influenced by it. Our history is long, and this makes our culture very difficult to understand. That said, I think that the advance of women, and women being equal, shows that China is developing, and I think most Chinese would agree that this is a good thing.

HENAN

November, 2013. Winchester, UK

Lavender was born in Luoyang city, Henan province, in January 1993. She spent her teenage years studying in Dalian, in Liaoning province, situated in the cold north-east of China. Her mother is a government official, working in accounts. Her father is a businessman, and co-ordinates several manufacturing plants. The UK is the first country she has visited. She studies Graphic Arts in the UK, the same as when she was in Dalian; her course has been split, with two years in China and two years in the UK.

How do you think future generations will view Chinese women in the early 21st Century?

Now, I think that life is better for Chinese women. For example, jobs are open for both men and women, not like the past, where some jobs only allowed men. Men could find more jobs. This is because in China women tended to retire earlier the men, to leave work earlier. Like my mum; because she is working for the government, she will get to retire at fifty-five. But the male employees have to retire at sixty. This is only for those who work for the government. But my dad can retire whenever he wants, when he decides.

Many young Chinese women wear clothes that would not be accepted in previous generations. Are these clothes accepted now? If so, why?

People accept these sorts of clothes now. These are products of the influences of western culture. From 1949 onward many women were influenced by western cultures, and they changed their fashion. Old people, though, do not accept this. Sometimes my grandmother doesn't let me wear this sort of clothing. I think this is because when she was my age, she was not allowed to wear these clothes. So she thinks I shouldn't either. The West's culture has been able to be so influential due to the development of technology. People now can watch videos of TV programmes from Western countries.

What do you think has changed most since your mother was your age? Do you think anything should change further?

My mother told me that when she was young she was not allowed to dance in public squares. This is common now, many old ladies like to do this, but back in the 1980s this dancing was private, and concealed behind a wall. It had to be done privately. You could dance with who you wanted. It is similar to now, but the kind of dancing people my age do it different! She went to university, which was rare. At that time many people lived in the countryside. Maybe their parents didn't have the knowledge about university and felt that their children should stay at home and work. But my grandparents did not live far from the city, and sent her to study. My grandfathers' brother was a university lecturer at the time, so they understood. The thoughts of my family were different to other families.

Do women have equal opportunities and rights now? For example, in the workplace, in school and at home?

I think women are treated equally now... but, have you ever been to Yunnan province? There is a lake called *lu gu hu*, which separates Yunnan from Sichuan. Near *lu gu hu* there is a minority people whose community is very different. In their community the man must listen to the woman, and the woman is in charge of affairs such as family and sex. But in the city, I think girls get the same opportunities. In education, in the past, in PE class we would just have running, but when I was in high school it had more on offer and you could do lots of different sports. Girls and boys can play the same sports and play each other. In terms of employment and salary, I think it depends on which jobs you choose. Different jobs pay different salaries. But if women and men choose the same jobs, I think they get paid the same. There are some jobs which hire only men; people who have to rescue those in danger, like firefighters, tend to be men. You need to be strong enough to rescue others, and women are weaker than men. In my family, my mother did the laundry but my father cooked. Because my dad is good at cooking, better than my mum! She isn't very good, ha ha!

In the UK and the US having a child out of wedlock is common. What do you think about this?

I think if a boy and girl have a baby together their parents will force them to get married. If they have a baby together they must marry each other. My parents know I would never do this, but if this happened to me, my parents would... well, I don't know! Ask me to marry the boy, or abort the baby; kill it before it is born.

Some people think that dating shows objectify and sexualise women for entertainment. What do you think? How do you think it affects the women (and men) who watch it?

I don't like dating shows, but my parents love them! At home, when the show starts, my parents call me and ask me to watch it... I don't know why they do this... I think it is just a show. In China, if you are a woman and you get on this show, they pay you 2000 yuan, I think, because my friend, who also studied in Dalian, attended a dating show. If she appeared on TV she would be given 2000 yuan. When I watch it I always think that the girls on this show have a good job, a good career, and I always wonder why they don't have a boyfriend. They are young, and look beautiful, and go to a good university or have a good job. I just assume that they are completely different when they wipe off their makeup. Normal girls struggle, but I don't see why these contestants do. That is why I think it is just a normal show, not really a reality show. I think girls wear makeup not just to attract boys, but to have self-confidence.

When it comes to dating, what do you feel is important?

I don't know what I'd look for; I have never had a boyfriend. I think the character, the personality, is important. I've really never thought about this… I guess I'm waiting for my dad to find me one, ha ha ha! He must be kind and hardworking, and I don't like boys who go to nightclubs and drink alcohol everyday… no playboys! And we can help each other in our lives. He must understand me. Or do my homework, ha ha!

In a relationship, what is your role? Are you equal?

I think we should be equal and should both work. I will do the things I like, and he can do the things he likes. We will respect each other. I think it is ok as long as what we earn combined can keep us going. We can put the money together.

If you could sum up Chinese attitudes to these topics in a few sentences, what would they be?

I think most Chinese would agree with my views. The most important thing to consider when answering this is what has changed. The change between old and new, the undeveloped and the developed. I think old people would not agree with my views. But people my age would. But some men still think women should stay at home and look after the babies. If a man is rich, really rich, he will not want the wife to work, but to stay at home and look after the family. But sometimes women work, not for money, but to do things they like and have their own life.

HONG KONG

December, 2013. Brighton, UK.

Zoe was born in Hong Kong in September 1992. She is an only child. Her mother is a nurse, and her father is a retired policeman. She studied since the age of fourteen in a boarding school in Surrey, and then went to Worthing college, and then to Chichester college. She is now in Brighton for her degree. She has travelled since she was small, sharing her parents' love of seeing new places; she has been all over mainland China, Korea and Japan before coming here. Initially, her parents had wanted to immigrate to Canada before 1997, and the whole family spent six months living there. They then attempted to move to the US, which also fell through. Eventually, they decided to stay in Hong Kong.

My mum actually told me I was adopted when I was thirteen. So I didn't know how to live in my family, so I told them I wanted to come here, to England. So I came here when I was thirteen, and got into a boarding school on my fourteenth birthday. But now I'm ok with that. My father was quite strict and I think, when I was little, he had wanted a boy and my mum had wanted a girl. They adopted me when I was three months old. When I was a kid my dad made me play basketball, football, and things like that. As for toys, I didn't get Barbies or anything like that, I'd get cars, a guitar, and my parents liked my hair short. When I went to nursery, I had to do swimming lessons, basketball, hockey, and triathlon. I still swim, and scuba dive… my mum made me learn the piano, the violin, ice skating, girly things. I did both these types of things at the same time. My dad was trying to make me like a boy, and my mum was doing the opposite, and they argued a lot because of this. When I went to high school in Hong Kong, my dad saw me grow up but wear shorts rather than dresses and he asked me 'Are you a lesbian!?' and I was like 'No! This is what you turned me in to!' It was then I decided to turn away from my dad, and do what I wanted to do. We didn't talk much anyway… he never let me touch him; I had my first hug this summer. But when I came here, when I was seventeen or eighteen, he started to talk to me as his daughter instead of not talking to me and ignoring me as he did when I was little. I'm a child of the nineties, and these parents spoil their children. Lots of kids don't know how to dress themselves, or how to wash, but my parents are older that these. And my mum is a nurse; for example, I got my little finger dislocated in basketball when I was little. It was at ninety degrees to my other fingers. My mum just came up to me and BAM! that was it, just like that, but other kids would have freaked out and cried but I never did that. I'm quite different from my friends. I went through this on my own, I am tough.

How do you think future generations will view Chinese women in the early 21st Century?

For Chinese girls now… I think that we get more respect than in the past. Chinese women are quite strong now, starting from older women and down to us, my generation. Girls can express themselves, but still the concept of how a woman should be and what a girl should look like is there. Like, sexy, but in a healthy way… but back then, this idea of 'healthy but sexy' could be dirty. It just depends on what people think sexy is. Like, if you wear really short shorts back then people will think you're a slut, but now people think it is normal, it is just how people have changed, and they accept it. But, for example, if you have your boobs hanging out of your clothes, that still is unacceptable. I'm not sure how people in the future will view my generation; it depends on whether they have an open mind on things. Nowadays people are quite open minded. Women are trying to be treated equally, but that's not going to happen, as we are not treated equally… well, I'm in Hong Kong, it is different to mainland, but if a girl hangs out with a guy, they expect men to pay. If they are fighting for equal treatment but doing this and that, expecting men to do all these extra things, is not equal. I don't think it will change much. But the thing is, in Hong Kong, girls are quite strong, and try to live without men, but that's the problem now. They are too strong and can't find the right man for them. So, that might get worse. I think it will be harder… now they see men as lower than before, and that is causing problems, and how women are treated. These tensions will continue.

Many young Chinese women wear clothes that would not be accepted in previous generations. Are these clothes accepted now? If so, why?

I think we accept these clothes more than we used to, but still, my parents don't care about this because I won't dress badly, but when I wear shorts they worry that I might get raped, they have this mind-set. Dads are dads. My parents know I have a boyfriend, but they won't say I have a boyfriend, they will say I have a 'friend'. They can communicate, but… my parents won't accept that I am grown up and have a boyfriend. They wouldn't accept me living with him; in my dad's view, if you live with a guy you are getting married. My mum has met him, and she thinks that as he is just a boyfriend, not a husband yet, I could still find someone else. She doesn't accept him because he is not rich, not clever. He is not poor, just normal. I know that parents want us to have a better life, but I won't choose a boyfriend just because he is rich or has a car. My mother would always ask why he doesn't have a car, but you don't need a car in Hong Kong! Back then, we didn't have magazines and stuff like that, but now we get magazines and Western and Chinese cultures are mixing up. The Chinese are absorbing the Western fashions. Hong Kong is an international place; we get lots of cultures mixing together.

What do you think has changed most since your mother was your age? Do you think anything should change further?

My mum was born in 1955; she is fifty-eight… so she was twenty in 1975. She is the youngest in a family of five. She is from Macao, and moved to Hong Kong when she was nine. My grandfather had been working there before the family moved across to meet him. My grandmother died when my mum was nine… my mum's brothers would work with my grandfather when they were young, but one of my aunts had to work, and quit school after primary school. They were poor. And my mum would cook for them when she was off school. She would learn to cook and clean, even before she turned nine. Back then, as soon as they were born, they were expected to help maintain the family. Nowadays, children are spoilt. My uncle also only finished primary school, but now he is a boss of a company. Back then you didn't need to be educated and have a degree. But now you can't do anything without a degree at all. We don't get that opportunity anymore; in Hong Kong a degree is not enough. And here, you don't have to have a Masters to get a job, but in Hong Kong if you only have a degree you don't get paid well, so you have to get a Masters. My dad tried to get me to do two degrees at the same time; you can do this in Hong Kong. It is so hard to be Chinese sometimes. I think women have changed their minds, the way they think. They think they are strong and clever; that has to change, they can't be that arrogant. Back then women had to know how to cook, but most of them now can't cook. They learn from books for their entire childhood, and their parents cook and do all this stuff for them. The boys, they are the same, their parents do all this for them. A boy who can't cook will go out with a girl who can't cook, so no one will cook when they grow up. Well educated, but they don't know how to cook! That won't work, and that is what is happening.

Do women have equal opportunities and rights now?

I'm here, so I don't know how it is in Hong Kong right now. If I said women aren't treated equally... well, my boyfriend works in the police in Hong Kong. So in front of his friends, his family, he has to act like a tough guy, and I have to act like I'm quiet and polite, and when he says anything I just say 'Yes'. But when it is just me and him he acts normal, and I can act normal. Every time I go back to Hong Kong I have to buy his colleagues chocolate and say 'Thank you for taking care of him'. I don't know if this is just the police. You gain face when people give you this, give you that. I give face to his colleagues, and he gains face from that. I don't mind if that helps, I think you have to do that if you get a better job from it. In my primary school we had eight girls in my class and twenty-something boys. Our English teacher used to make every one stand when he was disciplining the class, but the girls got to stay sitting… I think it's fair, ha ha!

In the UK and the US having a child out of wedlock is common. What do you think about this?

My parents have this traditional Asian mind; they think if you get married you are married for ever, there is no divorce. I was brought up with that. I accept having divorce, but not having babies without getting married. I mean, you could have babies *before* getting married, but not raising them on your own. They don't accept it, so I don't accept it either. I respect them for that. It is so hard not to think like this. My uncle got divorced because his wife cheated on him, so my dad (it was my dad's brother) said she was horrible and he could therefore accept the divorce. But my cousin's wife committed suicide because he cheated on her, but my dad was like 'Oh, he now has a new girlfriend, they are living together' and I don't know why… I think maybe he treats them differently because of the gender. It is horrible that my cousin did that… he saw her dying but didn't help at all. She took pills, and she threw up dark blood, and my cousin came home and saw it, and I don't know how but he got her to the shower, but then he left, so she is throwing up all this blood in the shower at home alone. And, I think she woke up and stepped on the blood, slipped, and died. That is what I heard. I don't know why my dad forgave my cousin. He is my mother's eldest brother's eldest son.

Some people think that dating shows objectify and sexualise women for entertainment. What do you think? How do you think it affects the women (and men) who watch it?

In Hong Kong we have these sorts of dating shows. The show, directly translated, means something like 'women in their prime', but it has the same pronunciation as saying 'the women left behind'. Quite clever, right? They're pronounced the same way, so a double meaning. It's so rude. The girls are like, maybe just twenty, so young, and they are considered the girls left over!? Twenty! I don't see how that is working. But, in that show, they are the ones the guys have to fight for, so they are stronger, the princesses, and they look down on the men, and pick on all these boys. But I don't think that is what a human should do, it's just so wrong. When I see these boys trying to win a girl, I wonder why on earth why these girls are treating these boys so badly. It think it's how they are brought up, and they were treated as princesses, so they look down on these men. These men have to impress them, just get their attention and things, but I think they shouldn't think like that. But because they were brought up like

81

that, and no one told them it is wrong, this is how they act. And they will be like that forever until they realise on their own. But on this show no one will tell them because it is what people wish to see. How on earth twenty years old is left out I don't know, I'm twenty-one! They are actually the ones who got themselves left out, by being like this. But they won't realise that until, I don't know when... if that continues in this generation, there may be social issues. I think Hong Kong girls are so hard to get, and I am Hongkongnese myself!

When it comes to dating, what do you feel is important?

I think my boyfriend respects me as me. I don't have to change my personality to fit with his. He respects me for who I am, and I respect him in return. I don't care about how much money he earns. He doesn't buy me many gifts, and I'm fine with that. On Valentine's Day I asked what he had got me. He replied 'Three words; Happy Valentine's Day' and I just burst out laughing. I just think that's enough. He didn't even Skype, he just text it to me, ha ha! That is fine, I'm cool with that, I don't mind.

In a relationship, what is your role? Are you equal?

I think he is the kind of guy that expects his girlfriends to clean up, he expects me to clean up and maybe do the cooking, but at the same time he feels thankful for it. If I do this, he is appreciative. In the future, if I earn more, other people may judge. He would lose face. If that happens, you don't have to tell other people anyway. But I don't have a job yet, I don't know how he's thinking. He gets around… £24,000 a year. Which, to me, is ok, quite good. And he gets more every year. But this is not enough for my mum; she will never be happy. You always want more when you have enough, you don't know how much is enough. But I don't have a job, I really don't know yet. I mean, I do illustration, and everything is Asia is about technology, design. There is no such thing as an illustrator in Hong Kong!

If you could sum up Chinese attitudes to these topics in a few sentences, what would they be?

My parents would have very different opinions to me. I think Hong Kong people don't know much about mainland culture. I think Hong Kong people would just accept this as the new trend. But my parents are of the older generation, they have old values, but people nowadays accept it. Hong Kong is such an international place, and it was part of the UK. When I was in Hong Kong, because I did the first two years of high school, I studied Chinese history, but in English. We studied the Opium Wars… and that was about it. I left for the UK before the modern stuff.

September, 2013. Plymouth, UK.

Jenna was born in February 1991 in Hong Kong. She has been in the UK for one year at the time of the interview. She lived in Canada for seven years with her father and his family after her parents divorced whilst he worked for an international IT firm before coming to the UK. Her mother stayed in Hong Kong as a housewife. Jenna attended primary school in Hong Kong, middle school in Canada, and high school back in Hong Kong. It was then that she decided to study in the UK for her degree. She studies Tourism Management.

I want to talk about my parents' divorce… it does affect me, in some ways. I want to get married someday, but this stopped me from thinking about it. When I'm in a serious relationship I don't even think about marriage. They have been divorced for four years; that's why I left Hong Kong. They were arguing forever, I don't know why. It just didn't work between them, even after my mother had my younger brother it didn't get better. But they waited until my younger brother was older. My mum seems a lot happier now, compared to then. My brothers still live with her, and it's where I stay when I go back to Hong Kong. I think this is why I can't think about marriage.

How do you think future generations will view Chinese women in the early 21st Century?

I can say that Hong Kong is more open, particularly compared to some parts of China. I don't know much about Chinese history though. I think now in Hong Kong it is really good for both genders, much better than before. It must have been horrible [in the past], I can't imagine that. I'm not sure how people will characterise my generation… education is important to girls now. We're trying to become more equal, and get the things we couldn't have before. In marriage, I wouldn't accept that a man would have other women. Loyalty and respect are important to me. And with money, I wouldn't mind paying the same amount with a husband in the future. If we had to pay the rent, I wouldn't mind paying half. And with kids, I think you should raise a child together rather than having the woman raise the child alone and have the man out earning money. Women of old could not work, or go out at all. Now it is different. We can go to school and get treated the same.

Many young Chinese women wear clothes that would not be accepted in previous generations. Are these clothes accepted now? If so, why?

I think the culture has changed, regarding fashion. It used to be restricted, and you could not show some parts of your body. One of the reasons is that you need to protect yourself from predators. Have you ever seen those hairy tights? Basically they are tights, but they have lots of fake hair on them. Women wear them in China at night to prevent some pervert attacking them. I think fashion has changed a lot. Because more designers make these sorts of clothes… but the way that Chinese women wear these clothes is, compared to the UK, less revealing. British women wear with a low cut top, you wouldn't see that in Hong Kong or China on the street. I think the shorts are ok… I have a few pairs of the little shorts! They are good in summer because it is so hot, because of the weather. But I definitely cannot wear this type of clothing if I'm going to my grandmother's house. She would be pissed off. So these are accepted in Hong Kong and China; just not around my grandma! I think they are accepted now because of influence from famous people. Both Chinese and Western stars wear things like this. And from friends. If your friend had really cute shorts then you would want them too. Movies and films too. The media, internet, especially now. Things are changing due to technology, I think.

What do you think has changed most since your mother was your age? Do you think anything should change further?

I think the main thing that is different for me, from my mum, is that I have the chance to meet more guys than she did. This was when I had returned to Hong Kong. My mother only ever dated my father, and she is still a housewife because my dad would not allow her to work. He would say 'Oh, you should stay at home and take care of the kids.' She never went to university or went abroad either… she went to secondary school. My mum has a younger sister and brother, and she gave the opportunity to them. So she stopped studying and began working to pay for their education fees. Because of the money issue, she never got more education. She came to Canada to see us once, but not when she was young.

Do women have equal opportunities and rights now? For example, in the workplace, in school and at home?

In the workplace, women tend to be in managerial positions in Hong Kong. And if your boss is a woman she would treat boys and girls differently. I think they treat guys better, maybe. I don't know why. I wouldn't say most women have better jobs than men, but some... over half. There are more female managers than male managers. Very different to mainland China! I think this is because women pay more attention to detail, more than men. And in school, it doesn't matter. We get the same opportunities. As long as you are a good student then the teacher will like you, it doesn't matter if you are a boy or a girl. If gender discrimination happened in Hong Kong my parents would sue the teacher. Like, when you apply for a job, write a CV, you only need to include your name and home address. That's all. You don't have to profile your gender, or your age. If an employer was to look at your CV and go 'You're a girl, I don't want you' it would be discrimination.

In the UK and the US having a child out of wedlock is common. What do you think about this?

Single parents can get a lot of money from the government here, can't they? I think, if it was me, I wouldn't want that to happen. I don't think it's best for the children. So women are more independent in Hong Kong... if a single woman is almost thirty then she might chose to use donor sperm, artificial insemination, and she would raise her child alone, without anyone else, because she is successful and she can chose to do so. She wants something related to her; a child, more than a pet. I don't think being a single mother would be a bad thing… if they have the ability to raise the child alone, then why not? They can give the opportunity to themselves. I think it's a personal choice. If a man gave up the responsibility, it is bad… if it is your child, why would you want to leave it alone? I think people would judge these girls in Hong Kong, give them 'a look'. Hong Kong people, as a whole, wouldn't agree with this. I would look, but I wouldn't say anything like some would. But a comment would be inside of me. I wouldn't say it, but I would think it. Maybe talk to my friends, gossip behind her back. I think many would give her a nasty look. My parents have never spoken to me about this sort of subject, about sex or relationships, but I can tell that if this happened to me, they would try and help me through it and support me. But I know some of my family would judge me. Like my dad's brothers or sisters. They would judge me. They would think that the baby would be a hindrance to getting me into university or a good job.

Some people think that dating shows objectify and sexualise women for entertainment. What do you think? How do you think it affects the women (and men) who watch it?

I think that some dating shows can damage the reputation of the women, the women on the show… or maybe all women. They could damage the way that boys see girls. Maybe, for my age, we know that if a guy is rich he can get girls. It is important to look good… for example, do you know Instagram? If there is a girl on Instagram and she wants more followers, she would post some photos, half naked or from a certain angle to make her look more pretty and get attention. Just for attention, I guess. To feel alive maybe? She wants people to look at her, she wants the guy's attention. Also, for guys, it shows that they need to look good to get the girl's attention. I think that there are different girls, who want true love rather than money. It would change the way men feel; you need to be rich, you need to be good looking… This sort of thing happens a lot in Hong Kong. Some girls go online to find rich guys; she would go on a website, type her name, her age, post up photos of herself and then post them online and wait for guys to contact her and chat with her and ask her for a date. And the girl would say, maybe, an hour date for HK$500. He would pay her for, just to go for a movie or a meal. She isn't a prostitute, it is just a date. Maybe he is a loner, and this how he meets girls. These girls, though, tend to be from not-too-affluent families and in want of money. But only for a movie or dinner. Maybe sex… you'd have to pay more, apparently. I watched a TV show about it. And I think this relates to the issue about single parents, and divorced parents. Because why would a girl do this sort of thing? Because of her parents! Most of the girls that do this are from single parent families, and do not see their dad, or their mum. I only know this from a TV show, but I think it is true. If you come from a good family, a loving family, you wouldn't do this sort of thing. But if you only live with your mum, and she is busy all the time working, and doesn't have the time to teach you about stuff, it would be influence from your friends which would change you the most.

When it comes to dating, what do you feel is important?

I think looks and personality are most important when it comes to finding a boy to date. Not amazingly handsome, as long as I find him attractive it is fine. He would need to be kind, to everyone as well as me. And he needs to have a good sense of humour; he needs to be able to make me laugh. He needs to be a gentleman; open the door for me, take care of me. In Hong Kong people seem in a rush all the time, and no one does this sort of thing.

In a relationship, what is your role? Are you equal?

I think we are equal in a relationship, I'm not a cook! If he was to cook, then I would wash the dishes. This is how we would work… half and half. I think it normal, for when we go out, to have me looking pretty next to him. I would do the housework… sometimes, ha ha! If I had a really rich husband I don't think I would ever need to work. But I wouldn't want to have to ask a man for money to enjoy my life and see my friends; I would need my own income. I think I would get a job then, I wouldn't betray myself, let myself down, for money. If he paid me to stay at home for the education of the children I would say 'No, why would I do that? Can't we just hire someone? Then we can raise the child together, rather than me doing it alone.' I would be ok earning more than him, but I'm not so sure... I think it is normal, it is equal. As I said, in Hong Kong many women earn a lot more than their husbands, and this is normal, so I do not think it will stop me.

If you could sum up Chinese attitudes to these topics in a few sentences, what would they be?

I think women nowadays in Hong Kong are lucky to be independent, certainly compared to some countries, like in the Middle East. We are free to be ourselves... we have the power to say something, even though we are women. We can petition the government, stand up for ourselves, and defend ourselves if we are in trouble. Like breast feeding, for example. When women do this in public in Hong Kong people give them a judging look, and after this happened a few women organisations went to the government and asked them to build them a room, a special room, in the metro for women to breast feed. And the thing is, men don't care about such things, because they are not the ones feeding the baby! But the women do, and we can stand up for ourselves and say 'We want this, we want this feeding room just in case we need to feed our babies when we are out.' And they wrote a proposal to the government and I think it is good we can do this sort of thing.

April, 2014. Chichester, UK

Celine was born in Hong Kong, and studied and lived there until eighteen, when she came to the UK. Her parents own a factory which makes handbags for designer brands, which are sold to Spain, Canada and Australia. She has been to Singapore, Thailand three times, Australia twice, mainland China, Indonesia, Okinawa, and now UK. She has been in UK two and a half years at time of the interview. Celine chose Chichester because 'the south of England has better weather', and Chichester has a smaller International School than most universities; Celine wants to make English friends, and learn more of the language. She studies music.

I think Hong Kong girls are sluttier. Do you know what I mean? They have more sex. I know lots of Hong Kong girls here who desperately want to date a Westerner, because they are different... maybe better looking, more muscular. Blue eyes, different hair. It makes me think that they are slutty. They chase Western boys. I mean, people like to try new things, but they get bored easily. I've been to nightclubs a few times in Hong Kong and I don't like it. But here it is better. People in Hong Kong like to go to clubs with loads of foreigners, and people always tried to take me there, but I always hated it. The Westerners there have this impression that Hong Kong girls are easy... when I was there a Yankee tried to pick me up and I told him to fuck off. He was offended, and got defensive, but I was like 'You were rude to me first!' you know what I mean? I was going to punch him. I have done that here before, ha ha! Some guy was trying to grab me in a club, and touched my bum. And what was I going to do? Say 'Oh, thank you'!? I punched him, ha ha! I don't know how we got this image, why people view Hong Kong girls this way. In Hong Kong girls who go to nightclubs are considered slutty, but here it is normal. They like to take photos, put them on facebook. Here it is normal, but in Hong Kong you look like a party girl. One of the girls that I went to college with there was really weird. Well, maybe not weird, maybe she just wanted to express her feelings. We were close friends. But when she added me on facebook she was like 'Why are you doing this? Why are you partying, drinking a lot?' It isn't her business, but I didn't say that… I wasn't doing what she thought I was doing, I was just having fun with my friends, do you know what I mean? She's quite an indoor girl; not boring, just traditional. I don't mind, it is fine, but she didn't have to say these things to me. Forcing her views on me, and being really aggressive. My mum knows [she is no longer a virgin]. Well, maybe she knows, but she pretends she doesn't know that I'm not a virgin. I don't know, she's never asked me… No, she asked me once. Whilst I was still studying in Hong Kong, she asked me 'What is the most intimate thing you have done with your boyfriend, just kissing or…?' and it was more than that… people here have facebook but they will just block their parents so no one can see anything. But my mum wants to see everything, whether it is bad or good, so I show her everything on facebook. I don't want to lie to my mum. She doesn't have the right to control me, but she has the right to know, she is just trying to look after me. So I don't want to block her, which would mean she doesn't know anything. Obviously, we are really far away from each other so it is important for her to know that I am safe and happy. She doesn't judge me, even in my first year; my parents just didn't say anything. But my dad doesn't know anything. Mum did tell me though, before I left, not to date anyone here. But it was hard to have, er, sex with my boyfriend in Hong Kong. The dorms are spilt, so boys and girls are kept apart. But I have friends who would have sex, a couple, whilst their roommate is asleep next to them. Same room! I thought that was disgusting! Imagine waking up to that, ha ha! A bit rude to ask them to leave as well... maybe bribe them, give them cigarettes or money if they clear off, ha ha ha! I lost my virginity when I was fifteen. It's ok, I don't mind telling you. I had been with him for two years before that. I mean, he was a good guy, at least he admitted after two and half years that he had fallen for someone else. He was honest, at least. I was like 'I don't want to share you with someone else, with another girl. You have to choose between me and her'. It was so weird, he is weird. I wouldn't want to be one of two. He couldn't choose, maybe he was scared, maybe he still loved me, I don't know. I told him to choose, but he didn't. So I stopped it, I stopped seeing him. After six weeks he called me at midnight, crying, drunk, asking whether I missed him. He was with the other girl at this time, and I told him he doesn't have the right to do this. He was with her for a few years, and when they broke up he tried to get me back. His mum really liked me, and she still contacts me, even now. We were close, me and his mum. She treated me like her daughter. As we were breaking up she said 'Even though he is my son, he really messed up. He needs to grow up'. The girl he left me for was quite traditional, you know? But she had many male friends, so that is a bit weird. Like me, easy going. But I am happy with cheap restaurants and stuff, I don't care. But his new girl likes expensive stuff. These girls have Prada at fifteen! So stupid, and they are so boring! I once dated a guy nine years older than me when I was... it was when I had finished my first year of university, whilst I was here. He was thirty, it was recent. He was from Hong Kong too, but we've broken up. Maybe [the age gap] was a bit much, I don't know. We were having dinner with his friends one night, I think we were in the car going *somewhere and I saw a bunch of flowers in the car; I knew that his friend was seeing a girl and I asked 'Is that for her?' and he replied 'Yeah, yeah', as we were having a meal with the two of them that evening. When we were having the meal my boyfriend asked them what they are doing, whether they are seeing each other and I said 'Of course, you saw the flowers!' but afterwards he took me aside and said 'You shouldn't have said that, because if he wasn't buying those flowers for her, but for another girl, you'd be screwing everything up'. And I was taken aback, you know? I don't fucking care if I ruin it, if this girl leaves him, I did the right thing, he shouldn't be cheating. He was like 'You shouldn't say anything at all about the flowers, if they're not for her it would ruin everything.' I was so unhappy. He was playing the whole I'm-older-than-you card, I really didn't like it. But I felt I should say it, it is how I was brought up. My mother told me to say what was on my mind, speak my mind. Even if I ruined the whole thing, he was cheating on her! But my ex-boyfriend didn't, he wouldn't. But he treated me really well. He paid for me to go to Australia to go and see him. Two months before we broke up, he bought me tickets. £1090 or something like that. It was my 21st birthday present. When we broke up my friends asked whether I was still going to Australia and I was like 'Hell yeah!' I loved it, I just didn't see him. I had nothing to say.*

How do you think future generations will view Chinese women in the early 21st Century?

I would say we have more… not power, but more opportunity to do what we truly want to do, rather than just listening to the family, or the dad or what their husband tells them to do. They are more independent, have more independent thoughts, and the way they think has changed. It is changing now. I mean, after another few decades it will be completely different. I think it has changed since I was young, in the last ten or five years. Because what I have experienced is different to other people. Those in mainland China may have different experiences, it depends on different factors. And if they come abroad, their lives will be different. You can always choose what you want to do, or don't want to do. But if you have a traditional family it makes it hard to change your life. They still are, inside, a baking-and-cooking-good-girl, but the factors affecting them have changed, the outside world has changed, so it is different for them. Outside events affect people. In Hong Kong and China, even though Hong Kong was colonised, we still had the traditional values and ideals that China had. People say that they [China and Hong Kong] are so different, but they aren't really. There are differences in education and stuff... Even though Hong Kong is more developed and has better education, in our minds we have the same way of thinking. I think that girls in Hong Kong are fussier than girls in China, but everyone is different! But all the girls here [in the UK], Chinese girls, are rich.

Many young Chinese women wear clothes that would not be accepted in previous generations. Are they now? If so, why?

I think that Hong Kong has been influenced, not even just by Western [culture], but also by Japanese or Korean. Many people love Korean stuff, get excited about Korean culture. It is so crazy, but it is all artificial. They do cosmetic surgery on their eyes, they look so different to how they should be. Their parents give them money when they turn sixteen, their parents actually encourage them to do this! It is good that you want your son or daughter to have a better future, but for me, it shouldn't be about the face… unless you're really ugly, ha ha! It is the choice of the person, up to them. But there shouldn't be pressure on them. You know, my mum tries to make my dad better looking. She always buys him cream and stuff, for his skin, but he can't be bothered, he never wears it. He says that he can't see the point; he is already married, he doesn't need to be good looking, ha ha! My poor mum! Ha ha! Anyway, sorry, back to the question, it is because of these foreign influences; they are everywhere! Korean, Western, Japanese, always on TV and in shops. America's Next Top Model, stuff like that. Foreign media, stuff like that. People do what they think is acceptable. Maybe some girls think it is acceptable to wear just a bra in front of other people, but those people [who see her] might not. Some Hong Kong people judge girls who wear tank tops; some of my friends would say 'Whoa, that's too much'… some people care about what others think, whilst some don't and just do what they want. Maybe they want [these clothes] because they see them in the street. When you see a beautiful girl, dressed beautifully, walking down the street then you will want to be like her. That is how fashion works! People don't care about whether they suit what she is wearing, they just want it. When they like something that much they won't think if it is suitable or acceptable. It is changing, fashion is changing. Maybe this style of dress is worn just once a week, when they go drinking, but for the rest of the time they are normal.

What do you think has changed most since your mother was your age? Do you think anything should change further?

My mum went to school, but not university. Her family is big. I have six uncles and three aunts, she was one of ten! And she was young, number seven I think. The older ones had to work when young, and the younger ones could go to school. I don't think she went to college, but she wasn't stupid, you know? So I got to go to university; that is a big change. And I have looked at photos of her when she was young and when she was in school and when she went out with her friends. She still dressed like a good girl, but I actually think we dress quite similar. Maybe the colours were darker, more dull, and obviously I wear clothes with less fabric, um, I wear less, ha ha! But the style is the same, the difference isn't very big. Well, maybe not now I am twenty-one, but our fashions when we were both fifteen were similar. Our fashions at twenty-one don't match though, not as much. I would wear a bikini to the beach, but she would say I'm showing too much, although I find it acceptable. If others can do it, why can't I? I liked the fashionable stuff. I wouldn't say it's a copy-cat thing, it's just the way the world is.

Do women have equal opportunities and rights now?

I think in Hong Kong women have an advantage over men for teaching, but for other jobs like marketing, men will have the advantage. But of course it depends on the person's character at the end of the day. I want to say we are equal, but deep down, I think men have the advantage. Men have more advantages in some sectors, because in these kinds of jobs you need to exert power and be in control. Some girls have these jobs, but I still have the impression of men having more power and having better jobs. It's the way people think, traditional values; whether they are considered equal or not, it is like this. But in school girls do better! I think teachers prefer girls. Boys are lazier and naughtier. Most of my teachers disliked me… I wasn't being naughty, I was just, er, energetic. I used to have to have meetings with my dad. Maybe I argued back, but I felt that I was just expressing my feelings and thoughts, and I ended up having a 'discussion' with my teacher. He didn't directly chastise me for speaking out, but he felt that as he was a male, and older, I should shut up. I felt that just because I am younger doesn't mean I am wrong, or that my ideas are worthless. My mum used to just cook and do all the cleaning, but now me and my sister have moved out and come to the UK, my dad helps. He has to! We used to, and now mum has lost us. I have friends, couples, who are living together… not many, at our age we can't afford a flat, but I know one girl who is living with her boyfriend in Lancaster, and she is a housewife girl, she'd do anything for a guy. But I'd be more of a half-half girl, you know? If I cook, you clean or if you cook, I'll clean. She does everything in the house, even for the other guy who lives with them. The other guy just lets her clean after him too! She told me that she even puts his pyjamas and stuff in the bathroom for him when he takes a shower, like a maid! And she buys him stuff! Her boyfriend is such a dick, and he is rude. He never acknowledged me in Hong Kong. She always defends him, say he's tired or whatever. I can't understand why she is with him. He treats her badly, but she still wants to be with him. I don't find that acceptable; if you love someone you'd do anything for them, but it works both ways!

In the UK and the US having a child out of wedlock is common. What do you think about this?

I remember that I had a friend who had an abortion after a year of being with her boyfriend. The baby was seven weeks old [when they had the abortion], and I found it disgusting to kill it, to end its life. I had a chat with her... our school used to have Sexual Education classes, and they told us that babies have feelings even when they are tiny, and they can feel what is happening to them. I think it is stupid not to have safe sex, and to end up having a baby! I mean, you can have an implant or something to avoid having a baby; if you're not prepared to have a baby, what is the point [of keeping it]? And if he doesn't use condoms, you need to be able to protect yourself! Implants, the pill, something like that. I mean, in my opinion, I don't think any guy cares much about babies. I don't want a baby without planning, just wake up and go 'Oh, I'm having a baby' without planning for it or knowing what you need. Money, education, providing for it or whatever. You made a person that has no future. It takes so much

100

attention and everything, but it's fine when you know what you're doing. If two people want a baby and they know what they're doing and they can afford it, then sure. That is fine. Marriage doesn't bother me much, I don't think I'll get married. Maybe I'll change, but now I think I'm not old enough, but it's fine to be with someone without being married… I don't know, I don't think marriage is that important for a relationship. You can have a perfect relationship without getting married. Maybe people get married, and they end up cheating on each other; there is no point of getting married just because you're pregnant. But my mum wouldn't accept it if I said I wanted to have a baby with a boy but not get married. People think you should get married, and after that have a baby, in that order. That is normally how it works, and she wouldn't approve of me having a baby without being married, but I think it is acceptable to do if you know what you're doing and you plan. If you just have an unplanned baby it's pointless, you don't know what you're doing, you think about the next step as you're taking it.

Some people think that dating shows objectify and sexualise women for entertainment. What do you think? How do you think it affects the women (and men) who watch it?

I haven't watched these. There is one in Hong Kong, but it isn't just about dating, it is a really interesting programme. It is about women, normal women, well, maybe older than expected-marriage-age… There is a term which is simply 'Hong Kong Girl' which means that all Hong Kong girls like guys to treat them like princesses and hold their bags, have more control and power in the relationship, be control freaks. Anyway, this programme finds these girls, who can't do anything, and they try dating guys they find unattractive but with similar levels of education and money. It's funny. They did sports on this island, like a date, it was funny. It really shows how these sorts of girls treat guys and how they act in relationships. I mean, it is really stereotypical, certainly for the girls... it can make Hong Kong girls look bad. There was a guy on the programme who tried to teach girls to use body language to attract men, but it was a load of rubbish. These girls can attract men, ha ha! Well, some of them are attractive, some not so much, maybe mid-thirties. And they are still dreaming about finding their prince charming. I don't think everyone in Hong Kong is like that, but it is funny to see that people like this actually exist! And there are some girls like this who are my age! Just early twenties and so useless! I mean, I can still cook for myself and manage for myself, but these girls can't even do that, their mother does everything! I am glad I wasn't spoilt.

When it comes to dating, what do you feel is important?

I don't really know... I don't think much before I date someone or have a relationship. He doesn't have to be rich or anything like that, middle class is fine, I don't mind. And as long as he doesn't speak like an idiot, doesn't swear a lot, that is fine. I don't like swearing. I don't mind if he is educated or anything, it is what is inside that matters. And I don't mind where he is from, these things are so superficial! As long as he cares for me and we can communicate, then that is fine. The only thing I don't like is guys who cheat. I had a guy who cheated on me and I broke up with him without thinking, even though I loved him very much. The guy who loved another girl, I mentioned him earlier. And that was that. That was the point I get to when I have been pushed too far I can't accept it, so I left. The end. So I don't care if a guy can cook or anything like that, he just needs to be fair and let me be free. Another of my ex-boyfriends said I could not talk to any guys, not even by text; he wouldn't let me go out, he'd always text and call me, making sure I went home alone. But before I met him I was single, and I'd only ever had one one-night-stand. My friends told me not to tell him anything I had done in the past that would lead to him forming a bad impression of me. But he had slept with loads of girls! Fairness, that is so important. He didn't trust me. Trust is important too. No point having a relationship with someone who doesn't trust you.

In a relationship, what is your role? Are you equal?

I just think that people should do what they want to do. Everyone has the right to choose their life. I've never lived with a partner, but if I did, I would do the housework as long as we take turns. Half-half is fair. I mean, if he is really tired from work I won't mind doing bits, but if he is like that all the time, that would irritate me. But he would have to do the same for me, if I was really tired. For most of my previous relationships we paid for our own food. We were students, we had no money! If I always expected him to pay for everything that would be so 'Hong Kong Girl!' That's what my mum taught me, you have to pay your way, you can't expect other people to pay for you! Special occasions are fine, he can pay, but if neither have much money what is the point? But when working, maybe I'd expect more. If there were things I really wanted I would just save up and get them myself! This makes sense to me. I did have a friend and he never allowed his girlfriend to pay for anything, he'd pay for everything, but he was a student! He didn't have much, so why did he offer? And why did she accept it? She should look after herself.

If you could sum up Chinese attitudes to these topics in a few sentences, what would they be?

I think most girls wouldn't have discussed losing their virginity or having one night stands [with me], they don't accept these things, even in Hong Kong. Most of the girls I know would think I'm slutty for having sex just once. Girls my age. They would think I'm slutty having just done it once. But I think that having sex in relationships is common. And the boys would have contradicting views. They like it when they can find girls in a club, but if it was a girl they liked or their sister, they would go mad. And if their girlfriend has a past, has done things, then they might not be able to see past that. It is more acceptable to sleep around for guys, maybe not for UK girls though, ha ha!

HUBEI

Xenia has been in the UK just one month at the time of the interview. She was born December 1990 and is from Wuhan, Hubei province. She studies Fashion Management in Winchester University as a Masters, having studied Business English at her university in China. Her family is a 'happy one'. She lived with her father and mother, and has a Chinese boyfriend waiting for her in China. They met in high school, and have known each other for eight years. Her mother is a businesswoman who sells magazines and books, and her father is a policeman. They both live in Wuhan. She has been to France, Italy and Sweden before the UK, travelling for one month and exploring.

I have just quarrelled with my boyfriend today, ha ha! We have known each other since high school… I was a transfer student to his school, and we were in the same class. He was a student representative for PE. He is good at running and sports, and is very good at basketball and learning skills like that because boys think it is cool. I wasn't too bothered as I liked another boy. Let's call him Tom. And my boyfriend now is Henry. So, I liked Tom, but Henry and Tom were good friends, like brothers. Very good buddies. They played together, lived together, good buddies. After middle school Tom and I came together, so when we were around seventeen years old. We broke up after one year. I had other relationships, but they were shorter. Then, when I went to

105

university, Henry called me. I felt some connection, so we remained in contact. But we don't go to the same high school anymore, we don't live in the same area, we don't contact each other so much. But we still knew each other. Often we would talk online, or text, but not particularly frequently. Because of this communication we become closer and closer, more close to each other and we knew each other more. The problem was that if he wanted me to be his girlfriend he had to consider how Tom felt. They are still friends, even better than before! When I was in third year of university Tom told Henry 'If you like her, be with her. If you make each other happy, then be together.' I still don't think Tom has found another girl yet. But then again, since we broke up we lost contact, and even now we don't really talk. It is difficult to make friends again, after a relationship… anyway, so Tom told Henry he is ok if Henry wants to be with me. So after the New Year's festival he asked me to hang out with him, in a group though. We went to a theme park. After that someone actually asked me why we weren't together, as we were such a great match. And he finally asked if I wanted to be his girlfriend, and I said yes! He is a decent guy; when he wanted to be with me he didn't have other girl troubles following him. I believed him, he believed me. He just had me. Sometimes I would find trouble with him, and think he doesn't care enough about me.

How do you think future generations will view Chinese women in the early 21ˢᵗ Century?

My family is good… I mean, a little bit rich. Rich enough to afford for me to study abroad and buy what I want, and I like fashionable things, I like shopping, I like spending money… But my boyfriends' family is not as good, as wealthy, as mine. It is… normal. An average family, in the middle. Not poor at all, just middling. And there is a problem here; he is a man, and I am a woman. Your boyfriend or husband must have more money then you, and buy you nice things. He must have a sense of pride. If I bought him something, which shows I am richer than him, he would feel hurt, insecure. I have bought things for him before, but I never mention the price. I always buy nice things like clothes and purses for myself too. I want to buy him nice things, not just things for myself. He never refuses, but I NEVER mention the price, ha ha! I always remove the price tag before I give stuff to him! He is working in a decorating company, decorating houses and selling materials. But the most impressive thing about him is that he didn't finish university; he didn't like studying, he just knows exactly what he wants. He just quit school, wanting to earn money, and he found a job. He just does what he wants, what he likes. He has a kind of personality trait that I lack. I just study because my parents ask me to. I'm not the kind of person with an exact goal, sometimes I'm confused with what I want. He has a vision, a goal, and I really respect that. So he can earn money by himself, which I can't, and he can do what he wants with his own money, and I can't. I want to be like him, and learn from him. I think it is essential to our relationship. And what he does, his actions, provide me with a sense of security.

Do women have equal opportunities and rights now?

I think that women are treated better in the workplace, more popular than before. There are many more men than women [in professional workplaces]. And they want female colleagues to chase! It is about being social… in school, I think it is almost equal. I can't tell any difference between how boys and girls are treated. In my university, the tutor always asked boys to do tough jobs, heavy work and lifting, as they are boys and girls should do gentle work. I think when I go shopping, or go out to play, the waitress or shop assistant always gives the bill to the man, never the woman. Because when I go out to eat with my boyfriend, they always give the menu to me and the bill to my boyfriend, ha ha! My grandma and grandpa told me that it was Chairman Mao who gave women their liberty. I think it's better for women now, better circumstances in China. At present, women in China are almost free to say and work and do whatever they want. This has been a big change for not just Chinese women but for China as a whole. More people think women should have the right to be equal with men. They are not equal yet, but nearly. The interesting thing is… my boyfriend told me that it depends on the occupation. There are some kinds of jobs which need women. Because women would find the job easier than men would. Things like secretaries and teachers. Another thing is that women can communicate better; maybe just in China, I don't know, but people will think 'You are a girl, you are not too busy to do this job' and if you are a beautiful girl, or a beautiful woman, and you are talkative and communicative, you can do well, and get a good job.

Many young Chinese women wear clothes that would not be accepted in previous generations. Are these clothes accepted now? If so, why?

Sometimes I don't like to see girls wear such short shorts. Because I think it is too sexy, is too over the top. And my parents, who aren't as fashionable as the younger generation, or older people like my grandma and grandpa, they will think it is not suitable at all. And it is not what a girl should be. If I wore them and my granny saw them she would punish me and force me to change. They are popular because you can see them in many stores; you can see them in the shops and malls, and in advertisements. Chinese stars and Western stars. In different movies, they are seen as cool. People want to look like film stars! Many different stars wear different styles, and many normal people want to be like them. People learn the style from them. If one girl does that, then maybe her friends will follow suit.

What do you think has changed most since your mother was your age? Do you think anything should change further?

My life is different from my mother's… when I wanted to change my laptop she told me 'You already have one!' because when she was my age she didn't have one at all! And when I complain I don't have beautiful clothes or about transport, that there are always [traffic] jams, my father would tell me in his age if you had a car you would be so satisfied. In his day you just had bicycles, and they were regarded as expensive, luxuries. Nowadays we have cars, but we are not satisfied with them. A new car, a bigger car, with a CD player, satnav, we want all these things. It is the industrial revolution, changing people's lives. For food too. Back then some food was rare. It depended on transport, weather, climate. Some people could not even get rice, get any food at all, and they were starving, but I still complain about food and say 'I don't like that, this is not good'. We need to be learn to be satisfied with what we have. My mother is not traditional, she never does the housework, and she is not good as a housekeeper. We have a housekeeper in China. Not here, ha ha, I must clean my own stuff! My mother is strong, she cares about her own business more than housekeeping things. But my father likes cooking, and he used to do the housekeeping when I was young and when we were not so wealthy; my mother would not, so he had to! He also helped me to get dressed and bought me things, which my mother never did. My family is special. My mother is not a traditional woman. She didn't teach me much traditional culture. She always told me I need to do what I want, and that women need their own money and should not depend on men. We should be strong inside and have confidence in ourselves and not rely on men, but have our own confidence. There are only your parents who can help you from start to finish. Boyfriends or friends may leave you, so you must rely on yourself. She never told me you must do cooking and cleaning, but I think she would have liked me to learn. What if I do not find a man like my father? If I was to find a traditional boy, I would struggle! Another thing I want to talk about is that my parents, and my friends' mothers, are quite different to my grandmother. They pay more attention to body and skin care [than the generation before them]. They spend a lot of time and money on beauty treatments and massages. They go to hospitals to get care like, er, Botox. To make them look younger and more beautiful.

In the UK and the US having a child out of wedlock is common. What do you think about this?

Single parent families are not common in China. I think it is important to get married. If you get pregnant before being married, your parents will think it is humiliating. Families care about the views of others... losing face, giving face. If you are pregnant but unmarried, what would people think? I am engaged, I will be married myself. I think it doesn't really matter. I personally will... several months ago... it is a bit private, but I think I will say; several months ago, my period didn't come. My mother knew, and asked me why I'm late. My mum was so worried. I repeatedly ensured her 'I'm fine, it is fine'. I have never told her I have sex with my boyfriend but she guessed, she knew. She thinks I did, but I always denied it. Because I didn't want her to worry. She asked me to have a test. I was scared too, but I didn't feel as if I was pregnant. But she pushed me and pushed me, and made me feel panicked. She made me buy the things, and do the test, and it said I was fine. But my mother did not believe it and still worried about my future because my period had not yet come. She told my dad what she was thinking, that I had had sex. And so my father was so worried! But he was not angry. It is always my mother who gets stressed out. She was worried I would not be able get married or study abroad. She does a lot of thinking, about things that I can't really contemplate. She thinks a lot. She thought if I was pregnant then I could not wear a beautiful dress

111

for my wedding. I am too young, she thinks. Finally my period came and she was released.

Some people think that dating shows objectify and sexualise women for entertainment. What do you think? How do you think it affects the women (and men) who watch it?

One of my friends was on a dating show, a beautiful girl. She went to find a nice boy, but she was just on the show once or twice, then she left. She found it boring, she said it is just a show, just a normal show which chases ratings. Some girls just wanted to be on there to display themselves so agencies and advertising agencies can find them. That is why she did it. She said you can choose what you wear; cosy clothes or a sexy dress, it is up to you. It depends on you. But you do need to do makeup, as it makes you more beautiful onscreen. She just wore a casual t shirts; she looked natural and cute. The girls just pass judgement on the men, and she will pick out aspects of his private life; lifestyle, interests, his previous relationships, his values about the differences between men and women. Lots of social questions are raised in this show, and it presents a lot of social issues for the audience to think about. China is developing quickly, and along with development a lot of social issues come out. My mother and father like these shows. They love to sit on the sofa and watch this. They think young people these days are so interesting, so different, to what they were like when they were young. I don't watch it, but I listen to their opinions; they always ask me what certain words mean, because some words are new and fresh words, maybe from websites and social media which they are not familiar with. But they are interested in these things. Some men are chauvinistic. If a man is a bit chauvinist all the women on the platform will criticise him, as they think he is not respectful, and is too full of himself. I think this sort of thing can empower women, although it is a bit fake. The interesting thing is that the man has the option to see a picture of the woman without makeup; most men choose to see the picture, as they cannot see the girl's real face on the show! Women just want to be good, look beautiful. I think it's a good thing, as they want to show their beauty to people, to the guy they like. I think it's fine if a girl can make herself happy, or confident, with makeup. Maybe not great for the skin, but it is ok. I never wear makeup, because I am a lady, ha ha! I think I look better without it.

When it comes to dating, what do you feel is important?

I think my boyfriend can do as he wants; he is strong, and I agree with him. He is good looking, but that doesn't matter so much. Of course I like good looking guys, but this is not most important. Personality is; he is charming. He has his own character… I don't know why I like him. He is trustworthy. My ex-boyfriend used to play with other girls, as he is really handsome. Henry is not bad though, ha ha! I don't care about his education, or *guanxi*.

In a relationship, what is your role? Are you equal?

He cares about who earns the most money, but it is ok. He knows the money I have I did not earn by myself. He has the ability to earn his own. I would take care of the house, of course. I feel it is my duty to do these things. Even though my mum doesn't do these things, I think it is part of my duty and I like cooking, I like to stay in the kitchen and cook different food. If I don't get a job I am happy to stay at home and take care of him. Of course I want a job, a decent job, but if I don't that is what I would do.

If you could sum up Chinese attitudes to these topics in a few sentences, what would they be?

I think that in my parents' generation, in that generation, people changed. Changed through this new global culture, a kind of global culture, and became more open, more than my grandparents. At least they agreed and allowed me to study alone, abroad, and travel around Europe. When I went to Europe, many people saw me and thought I was too young to travel. I was nineteen, but I looked younger than that. Many people thought I was too young and wondered why my family had let me travel alone. Many people were curious of me! Even my relatives thought my parents were crazy to let me travel alone. And my friend's parents, they are also open. Many of them study abroad and travel the world, see different places and meet different people. They think it is good to open my eyes, broaden my horizons. I think it is a good thing. This was an impossibility for them at my age.

JIANGSU

October, 2013. Birmingham, UK.

Penny was born in July 1990 in Lianyungang city, Jiangsu province. Her true date of birth is actually in August, but her family received their certificate late, as she was not born in a hospital but her grandmother's home. She has been in the UK for one month at the time of the interview. The UK is the first place she has travelled abroad. She studied in Xi'an International University, studying International Economics and Trade. She is now studying at Aston University; Finance and Investment. She has a large family; mum and dad, two stepmothers, and their children. Her mother was her father's first wife, and he has subsequently had a further two. She has one step brother, who is in primary school. Her mother is a housewife, who used to be a part time sales woman. She gave it up to stay at home. Her father is in the construction industry. She lives with her mother and she meets her father fairly regularly.

How do you think future generations will view Chinese women in the early 21st Century?

I think that besides the countryside [in the cities and towns] girls are freer than before. They can have an education, but in the past, they had to work for money to pay for their brothers. Also, I think girls, lots of the girls I know… many of their parents spend lots of money on them to acquire talents, like playing the piano, instruments, sports, calligraphy, things like that. They invest in their daughters. Before, Chinese parents would not do this. Also, many lucky girls like me have the chance to go abroad, to experience different cultures, a different life, and to live an independent life. I think these are big changes. I think around this time has the first generation of a Girl's Revolution. For the first time girls can actually, in the 21st century, bring change from the old society to the new. They can ask their parents for dolls when they are little, and now they can choose their own boyfriends and husbands. Their views can be accepted by their parent, and the parents consider how their daughter thinks. This is the first step for future girls to be freer and more equal in future times.

Many young Chinese women wear clothes that would not be accepted in previous generations. Are these clothes accepted now? If so, why?

I think that we don't totally accept these new revealing fashions; just partially. My father would not allow me to wear these short shorts. I must wear trousers to below the knee. Other girls may wear strange clothes, strange styles, and most Chinese are ok with that. Parents don't like it, but we want to be happy and free. I think they are more accepted now because after our country opened its doors to international influences, many people come from the West and different countries, and they change the people they meet. Like in international cities, like Shanghai. They change the people they meet, and their views are very modern compared to other

Chinese. And maybe these Chinese affect the other people around them, it spreads. It's fashion! Maybe the young parents are very open in their adulthood, as they were teenagers during these years, maybe they will allow their daughter to wear these things. These younger people accept these things.

What do you think has changed most since your mother was your age? Do you think anything should change further?

My mum often tells me, when she was my age, around twenty, she was working in a factory making her own money. But I am spending her money! She always said that when she was young she always did a lot of work; my parents came from the countryside, and she didn't get a chance to finish her education, she just finished her primary school education. So after primary school she went to the factory, maybe a five hour commute… it was assigned by the head of the commune. At that time there was a 'big leap' in China. She always told me to be tougher, to save money, don't spend without thinking and things like that. My mother and I have a totally different view on strong women. My mother and I have totally different views on strong women, like Hilary Clinton, women who work as leaders. Maybe female doctors, females CEOs, they really work hard and their own life is a little boring, and many of them do not have time to have a boyfriend and marry. She told me I cannot do that, I must find a boy and get married when I graduate from university. She thinks women should lay their lives on men, that women should spend their husband's money after they get married, lead an easy life. Have children, raise them, and then their life is complete. She thinks that's the perfect process of life. She has not remarried, she has had partners before but they have both failed. The thinks her second partner could not provide well enough, and could not make her happy. As she had a family before, because she has me, it is hard for her to find a lifelong companion. My mum wants me to marry, but I am studying a degree, which means I want more from life. I want a good career; I want to make a lot of money. I want cool work, something different and challenging, not just sit in an office every day. Maybe get some promotions, climb the ladder, and just succeed. I want success. Maybe marrying a boy will affect my ability to do so; I told my mum I won't let a week's wage slip by to sort out a lover. She refused to talk to me, ha ha! Different values… maybe a lot of women get official jobs, and can do better than men at this level. Women do better than men at team leader or CO levels, especially in sales. A woman can actually get these jobs! Before now, women could just do labour, nothing where you must use your mind. No white collar jobs. Many leaders now are women, much more than before. Many men actually feel threatened by this, particularly in the US. Also, women can accept things like divorce must easier now than in the past. In China, they would feel shame and people would consider her worthless. But now, they can continue their life; maybe start a second life…

Do women have equal opportunities and rights now?

I think it depends on how you interpret the word equal. If we really treat women equally, men should not give way to women, or let women go first. Men can compete with women on everything; *that* is equal. Many women shout for their equal rights, but at the same time they want more from men, to let them go first. I think it's a contradiction. In school, girls and boys are almost equal, and teachers often like girls more than boys because boys are annoying. Boys play around, whilst girls like to study hard and make their grades higher. Most scholarships go to girls. In the work place I think girls still cannot get equal rights. Many businesses will explicitly advertise for men, so many jobs. Construction jobs need logical thinkers, IT companies, and they prefer men. Even if they don't express 'we don't want women' when they receive CVs they will just throw away female candidates' CVs. It is easier for men to get promotions than women.

In the UK and the US having a child out of wedlock is common. What do you think about this?

I don't understand why women would have a baby without a husband. I think most of them had a tough teenage life, maybe 'party girls' and maybe their boyfriends are irresponsible and do not want to take the responsibility of the baby. I think it's bad. In a way, maybe they choose to raise their baby alone and not give up is strong, but I can't understand it. Many single mothers are so young, and they limit their own lives, their own freedom. They must sacrifice much of their passion and energy for the child. I would never do this, I know that.

Many women think that dating shows objectify and sexualise women for entertainment. What do you think? How do you think it affects the women (and men) who watch it?

Some people think this show makes women look bad; for one man to select a girl from a bunch of girls. And these girls will say rude or personal things to the man who came to find a girlfriend. They say it is just joking, just pretend, but I don't like it. It is just a play, just for fun, or entertainment. When I'm eating dinner, I need something to watch, ha ha! I don't know why there are shows like this, almost every channel has a dating show. They will always find women who wish to participate. It spreads a bad view about marriage; the women, most of them are very frank, they just say 'I want a rich older man', they just like these sorts of men. Young women chasing such older guys. All the women on it express views which could not be aired in public... most of the women lose interest when they learn about the man's background, career, social status etc. if these things are bad; if they don't match the woman's standard, she will lose interest. It makes many girls think they need to find a rich partner. Maybe some girls have this thought, but they do not act on it, but after this programme comes out, they speak it out loud, they thinks it's fine, they think it's good. I was emotionally moved by this, as many of my friends and family have told me 'You need to find a boy who is good, at least equal to your family.' It's a common thing, but the programme has pushed it, made it so acceptable. And these programmes are so popular; it really has the ability to affect people's views.

I think that it has become too extreme; for example, it really affects people's thinking. It makes men want a beautiful girl to gain social status amongst their friends. They tell people that it is normal and right to find a partner who has a similar status. So for those who do not have their own view, who are often influenced by other, it can be damaging.

When it comes to dating, what do you feel is important?

I have never had a boyfriend. I really don't know what kind I boy I'd really like. I don't know what is 'love', actually, and I just like handsome boys but when it comes to a serious relationship, I don't know what to do. I'd want him to be hard working… the standard of seeking a future partner is finding one with good humour and with the prospect of success in the future, and can take care of me well, make me feel safe. I am girly, ha ha, although I said I am a strong woman, ha ha! That is the standard I want, but a mature view of mine is to find a quiet, handsome boy who can play music. When I was young I learnt painting, and my teacher really thought I had potential, and he wanted to be my tutor, to develop me. But when my dad saw the students were painting a naked woman, he took me away, he didn't want me to do that, and I had to learn piano. I was young, naïve! My art life died then, about thirteen years old.

In a relationship, what is your role? Are you equal?

I would want to be his soul mate, and at the same time I want to be a responsible wife to support the family. Earn money, and if we have a child in the future I won't abandon him or her because of my job or something else. If my husband wants me to look after the child, I will not disagree with him. I would want our love to last long. I wouldn't want our relationship to change. The role for him would be that he is never bored. I couldn't be with him all the time, every day. We would have our own lives. If he wants to be free and independent I will still love him. I like babies but I don't want to have one on my own. I don't want to give birth myself, maybe adopt. Many people say Chinese women are not independent, they are weak, but they do a lot. People can't imagine. My friend told me once that her mother was holding her as a baby on a bus when it crashed. Everyone fell down, but not my friend's mother. She would not allow harm to her baby. She was the only one who didn't fall over.

If you could sum up Chinese attitudes to these topics in a few sentences, what would they be?

All these things we have discussed have happened in a short time. We haven't seen the process of change. Before we opened our door to the internet world, we were very conservative, but after we are affected by Western culture we feel everything is fresh and we want to try it. During this process we think many things, not necessarily the wrong way, but in different ways. We didn't feel the gradual factors that implement this change. When we wear short shorts or leggings, we feel normal, every girl wears this, and we don't feel sexual.

122

We just didn't notice the change. We just accept it; we don't think it's bad. And because our government is so corrupt, many people go abroad. Most of these people are actually children of government officials and businessmen. Harvard University etc. but most students who don't go abroad are trying, they have the American Dream. I had the American Dream, it brought me here. We get affected easily, as we experience things we could never even think about before.

August, 2013. Southampton, UK

Ivy was born and raised in Suzhou, a city near Shanghai, famous for its botanical gardens. She is studying a degree in fashion in Southampton University, having arrived just two months previously. It is her first time to leave China. She enjoys painting and drawing and playing computer games to relax after her studies. Her father is a businessman, dealing in art ware and materials. Her mother is a housewife, after retiring early after an accident that left her unable to continue working. She was born in December 1989.

In the period where my father was a little child all the Chinese were very poor, and the policy was that no Chinese can do business, but my grandfather did. He was considered 'poisonous'. This led to my grandmother and grandfather to have a divorce. In that period it was very shocking, and not many accepted it. My father had to live with his grandparents. It was not common to have a divorce, and no one could accept my grandmother. She had little contact with my father. Later, she found another man and remarried. Because of this my father was very lonely and no one paid attention to him, except my mother. But my mother's parents do not agree to my parent's marriage because my father has no dad in their mind. They think his family has no happiness, and is very unfortunate. They didn't want them to get married. But at last they had me! Before they got married my mother's parents gave my mother a rope and said 'If you get married with him you are dead to us'. Very, very cruel, mean. They told her to commit suicide if she married him. They were very mean to my father in that period.

I know my mother's parents, but we are not that friendly, not that close. Especially not my father and my mother's family.

How do you think future generations will view Chinese women in the early 21st Century?

I think now things like concubines are not liked by society, but there are still many. I think it is not good too and the whole of society dislikes this. Some men who are very wealthy and have a lot of money can have many women. I think women are freer now, but there are still some cases of unequal treatment. I think they are freer now; they can find a man, whether he has a family or not. She can control her own life, and it doesn't matter. Perhaps others will think is not good, but it doesn't matter.

Many young Chinese women wear clothes that would not be accepted in previous generations. Are these clothes accepted now? If so, why?

In the past girls had to cover their body, but now we have more education and now we have access to foreign media, and now the things outside China and become more open. They can do more things, and can touch the world outside and make friends. Now it doesn't matter who wears short tops. I think foreign things and the internet have caused these things... maybe TV, more social activity...

What do you think has changed most since your mother was your age? Do you think anything should change further?

The biggest change since my mother was my age is that when she was my age she was already pregnant with me! This is the biggest change; I am twenty-three, I have no boyfriend, no baby. My parents may say 'Hurry up, find a boy' but it doesn't matter. They think I should find my love by myself. They wouldn't mind if he is Chinese or not, it depends on myself, and if I love him. I think this is because I accept education, but in her time she had already got a job, and had no education. She only graduated from school, with no further education. But I am still in education.

Do women have equal opportunities and rights now?

I think women are treated equally now, but it is still a little bit unfair. For example, in my home, my mother does all the housework and my father does nothing. When I was young, my mother worked too. She had to leave due to an accident… but even when she was working she had to clean the house and cook the food and look after me and my father relaxed. Also, if you are a girl and you are in the street, and you are alone, thieves may come up to you and take your bag, your things. But if you are a man, they won't do that. Because the man is stronger, and they think women are weak and they can take things from her. Another example would be in the workplace. If you are a girl, maybe you will just do writing, or some job like secretary. But if you are a man you can do lots of things, and become a manager. Female managers are not as common as male managers.

In the UK and the US having a child out of wedlock is common. What do you think about this?

I don't really mind about single families or these things, but I think many Chinese would not agree. It shows they are not traditional, if they have a baby and they divorce. The woman may have to find another father figure for the baby. My parents would not allow me to marry a man who already has a baby, and has a past family, I would have to bring up the child, be the child's mother, but the child is not mine. They would think it is very unfair to me, that it is not good. But I think it is ok if I love him. I think the younger generation think it's ok.

Some people think that dating shows objectify and sexualise women for entertainment. What do you think? How do you think it affects the women (and men) who watch it?

I think these dating shows are bad. If I was to simply see you, I could tell that you would be suitable as my future husband. I think that feeing would come over a long time, mutual agreements, not over a show, with just a few words exchanged. Dating shows focus on superficial things; if the man has money, then women remain interested. If he doesn't, then they lose interest. It isn't love, just 'picking vegetables'. And to be honest, I've never seen these shows. I think they're boring and a waste of time. I don't really like any entertainment shows…

When it comes to dating, what do you feel is important?

I think the most important things when dating is to have mutual interest, and to have talking topics… and he should be a gentleman! He must take responsibility for the whole family, not be like a child. I shouldn't have to take care of him, he should be self-sufficient. I think he can be wealthy, but if he has no money it doesn't matter. The ability to earn money is ok, if he is skilled and a hard worker. But if he has no money and no education and no skills then I think it isn't good. He will not be able to look after a family.

In a relationship, what is your role? Are you equal?

In a relationship, I think my role is to pay attention to him and help him with his job and his life. And take care of him after work, like cook food for him, whatever he needs. Even if I think he should look after himself, I will look after him. I think I would like to work when I am married, as I think if women get married and have no job then I think she can be weak. She will not be able to have a say about money.

If you could sum up Chinese attitudes to these topics in a few sentences, what would they be?

Summing up Chinese culture is difficult. I think a small majority of Chinese girls are traditional, and get married at an early age, maybe just twenty years old; they graduate high school or college very young, and don't want to go to university or can't afford. They are very traditional. These girls are more likely to get married and have a baby young, but most Chinese girls will work if they do not go to university. They will work, then find a husband and have a baby. Many of my old classmates have babies now. When I am on Chinese social networks, I see many photos of cute little babies. It think they are very traditional. I don't know if in the future they will divorce... I think it is too young. But I do think that a small majority marry young and settle down young. In China most girls who are around twenty would find a boy who is older, maybe five years older. I think because they are better at taking responsibility; they already have money and a flat, and know society well and can look after a family better.

April, 2014. Southampton, UK.

Shirley was born in Jiangsu province in October 1991, and studied in a Shanghai university for four years. She has been in Southampton for three months at the time of interview. She has never worked, but always given her time to her studies. When not away at university, she lives with her parents and both her grandmothers. She has been to Japan, Taiwan and the Philippines before, as well as all over China, sightseeing, having fun and eating with friends. Her father is a teacher, and her mother a house wife.

Something that you might find interesting is how we think about girls with PhDs. Because it is always thought that females with a PhD is the third type of person; the first is male, the second is female, and the third is female with a PhD. I think maybe nowadays there are more girls who are educated with a PhD than men, usually because girls tend to be harder working and boys want to leave early and go to work. So girls now are more enthusiastic about PhDs. Boys, at home, don't want their girlfriends to be too clever, too educated. This is why female PhD holders are the third type of person; they cannot match anyone! It is so hard to find a decent boy. It is hard for them. To find a boy as educated and clever as them would be very hard… if I do one it will be after marriage!

How do you think future generations will view Chinese women in the early 21st Century?

The communists made the law that one man can only have one woman, and before this many men had several wives. I think these women were viewed as less, as lower than men. This happened under the Guomindang, the Nationalists as you call them. So bad. And in ancient China, in the Qing dynasty, this was more common than under the Guomindang. So you see, it gets less. Things for women are getting better. I think girls, now and in the future, will vary. There will be different types of girls, you see? Because from 1949 onwards women became valued more; and there is the one child policy. No matter if you are a boy or a girl, you are the apple of your parents' eyes. You are their treasure. So girls are raised the same as boys. There are many types of boys, with different characters, different destinies. And now this will happen to girls too! We are different, independent, and unique now. With just one child, the girl is treated like a princess, and has her own education and own thinking and her own life. Mao said that 'Women hold up half the sky' and I think that we have great abilities, great potential. We are equal, as some things we can actually do better than boys.

Many young Chinese women wear clothes that would not be accepted in previous generations. Are these clothes accepted now? If so, why?

I think that in the old times, we couldn't wear these things because of culture, because Chinese civilisation had been seriously affected by Confucius, by Taoism, this kind of thinking. And these ideals put a lot of emphasis on *fu de* which is, er, virtues. Virtues of women, you see? It was not good for females to remarry after her husband dies, and it is forbidden to wear dresses too short, too sexy, it was forbidden. But during

Mao's period, people's thinking was not so affected by Confucius, but by the time. The revolution, their own ideology and thinking. You know, because China had changed from being colonised and invaded by other countries and women then, because Mao encouraged women to have power, to have value, felt they were lifting up half the sky! Women in this period have a very strong will to prove to Mao that they are strong too. And during this time the women's clothing is the same as men's, not beautiful. And since then Deng Xiaoping created his open door policy so the clothes and opinions have changed a lot. We like fashion; we usually watch fashion shows on TV or on the internet in Milan, Paris and London, and it is so cool. And we like it, so we wear it. And our parents encourage us, because they love us, we are their only child, they want us to be happy and beautiful. When they were young they didn't have these kinds of fashion and clothing, and they want us to wear what we want freely. I mean, my mum even encouraged me to bring a bikini to UK! I even wore it in Beijing! And when I was in the pool or on the beach in the Philippines. Because all the girls are wearing bikinis; if you wear too much you'd look funny!

What do you think has changed most since your mother was your age? Do you think anything should change further?

So many things have changed! Food, transport... But as a woman... She couldn't wear this kind of clothing [Shirley is wearing demin shorts] and another thing is she was not free with boys... I mean, she could have male friends, but women were shyer, shyer than in our generation. Shy is like… well, if I accidently touch you I could just say 'Sorry' but back then they would be embarrassed, and say 'Oh! I am so sorry! I didn't mean to!' There are still girls like this, but less than when my mum was younger. And obstacles to university are much fewer; for the entrance exam, it doesn't matter. No matter what your family background is or your gender or whatever, anyone can attempt. If you reach the marks, that is fine, you can get into university. No matter boy or girl. And for me, I think there are still some problems in the job markets, especially since the 2008 global recession. I mean, my major is about shipping. It is easier for boys to get jobs than girls in maritime industries. Because boys are better at marine things than girls. You know, being on the ships can take three months. On container ships. A very large ship but a crew of just twenty. I think it is understandable for men to be on this, not women! But those who deal in logistics, broking, it is easier for men too. It is because men can drink. The drinking culture is very strong in Chinese business, and boys can drink more than girls. It is a male dominated industry. It is normal for the boss to consider gender. I mean, girls can become pregnant and will have to leave their jobs, and there is a law allowing women to have this time off for the baby, and have it paid, so bosses don't like the risk of hiring women. To hire a man is more profitable, especially over young women who will be getting married. And especially after 2008.

Do women have equal opportunities and rights now?

Well, in my family my dad is a good dad, a good husband. My mother doesn't know how to cook, it is always my father. I think I am shaped by my parents. My mum doesn't know how to cook, and at Chinese New Year when my father wants to go and play cards with his friends and drink, he would cook soup and make Chinese bread for my mother, and leave the hot soup in the pot and take the bread to the bedroom so she can have breakfast in bed, and when she wants more she can just reheat the soup. And when he goes out for dinner with his friends, if he finds something my mum likes he will bring it back for her. Some of his friends think it is a shame to take the food to a wife, but for my father it is ok and he loves her. He always does this! My father earns a lot more than my mother, but he leaves his bank card at home with her; I think she controls the money for the whole family. This makes me think that my husband should treat me really well, otherwise I will break up with him! My father is a good example, and my parents are a good example of what I want my marriage to be like.

In the UK and the US having a child out of wedlock is common. What do you think about this?

I don't know how I think about this... you know, it can be separated into different types of relationships. I mean, my tutor here (I am not sure if this is true) said that he is in a relationship with another tutor, and they are not married, but they have a very cute boy. The thing is they love each other, and they don't need marriage to maintain a strong relationship. They are strong enough! Love is strong enough for them. This is good, not bad, it is their belief but they are still like a family. It won't affect the child. But maybe, when people get drunk and have sex and then have a baby, this is bad. This is irresponsible. This will have a bad impact upon the baby. He will not have a father! In China, less people are married now than before. One thing I think that isn't good, in China, is that young couples get married and have a baby and then they realise they are not suitable for each other and break up. This must be hard for the child. Like, together with a baby and then they realise they don't love each other and have a divorce. This is so much worse than just not getting married in the first place. It is important to get to know the person first, to decide whether they are right for you, and then get married later. You should consider the relationship before bringing a child into the family. Divorce rates are getting higher and higher... I don't know why.

Some people think that dating shows objectify and sexualise women for entertainment. What do you think? How do you think it affects the women (and men) who watch it?

I think it has changed. At first, when this show first came to China it was very hot, and every family would watch it. At that point, it was because all the women were so beautiful, and so highly educated, some were CEOs, and everyone liked them. They had good abilities. Buy why can't they find a guy in real life, why does she come on the show? So people started to think like this, and asked what kind of boy they want. I think it is very different to the British version. In China all the

135

boys are different. They are picked. Some are educated, some are not but with a good salary, it is very interesting. In our programme the girls have more power than the men, the girls judge the boys and evaluate the boys. The girls choose more than the boys. It is very interesting to see strange boys go on the shows and be picked on by girls, have their bad points picked out by these women. The show just wants to attract people. They arrange for strange boy or strange girl, it is funny. That was in the beginning. But now, people think it is just a show, not real; out of 100 contestants just two or three are real. My mum always watches them to find boys suitable for me. And the women who watch it value boys, they are thinking about the boy, judging him too. And which girl is suitable for him, or whether their own daughter is suitable. Another impact is that my mum wants to pick an ideal boy for me, so she takes qualities from all the different boys and mixes them together, so this boy, my apparently perfect boy, doesn't exist! Ha ha! Handsome, rich, polite, good character, healthy, happy, kind hearted, respectful, good virtues, ha ha! Tall, good looking, light skin (we like light skin) good job, decent salary, good family. But, in reality, it is just ideals, it is just a joke. Impossible. Similar to Korean dramas, similar story, ha ha! I think men are less interested in this sort of show, mainly women watch it. When my father watches with my mum, on the one hand he is always wondering 'Why are these beautiful women on a show to find a bloke?' And the second thing is that he is also trying to pick an ideal guy for me, like my mum!

When it comes to dating, what do you feel is important?

To speak frankly, when I first meet a boy, first impressions are important. Appearance and height. For me, I am not asking too much... I think 170cm is ok. He must be taller than me when I am in heels. I don't care if he is super handsome, he just needs to look clean and that he takes care of himself. Clean, hygienic, smart. That my boyfriend is really nice to me, that is important. His personality, yes, that is important. A good temper, not easily angered. Not picky about things, the same as me. A casual life, a casual attitude. Not so picky. Money isn't important, not now, I am young. But money is good, the more the better. If he is normal, that is fine. My boyfriend is on the same level as me, and his family can't afford a flat in Shanghai or whatever. Studying here is very expensive. So when I go back and get a job I will work hard and pay back my parents. So I hope he and his parents can afford the mortgage, to pay the deposit, and then I will help him, and pay my share after I have repaid my parents.

In a relationship, what is your role? Are you equal?

He would pay for me. I think that this is normal in China. If you go for a date in China and the boy asks you to pay, this is strange! For me, and for many of my friends, when we feel that our boyfriends are short of money we will pay, but he would always offer. I never cook for my boyfriend, ha ha! He can't cook though, so I guess if we get married I would have to learn. He says he will clean the dishes, wash everything for me if I cook, so that is fair, ha ha! I don't really bother with makeup; if we are together for our whole lives, he needs to be aware of my bad sides. If he only sees my good side, all my good qualities, what will he think when we are married!? When he sees me very tired or without makeup or something! I let him see me like this now; not bad, just not with lots of makeup and perfume. Just normal. I don't want him to think I'm perfect. Before we will get married I think we will live together, and have sex. Marriage is important to me; shortly after marriage we will have a baby, maybe just one or two years after. So it is important to get to know everything about him. So living together, and sleeping together, is important. I need to know. It is better to know before our marriage whether we are suitable or not. Live together first, and *then* see if it works and get married and have babies. This is a big change from the past. Many girls think like this now, living together, but in the past very few did this. They just got married, and then realised they clashed and had to change to adapt for each other. Very difficult, but in the past this is so common. In the past, when people lived together only after marriage, the divorce rate was very low. Like my grandparents, both sets. It is strange actually, I don't understand the pattern. And my great grandparents had like a blind date, their parents set up their wedding, and they never met before. They had no option. But they had good life and good relationship. Harmonious, I think you say in English. The divorce rate was so low at that time, but now is so high. Everything has changed! If marriage can't maintain the relationship, the love, then divorce is the best thing.

If you could sum up Chinese attitudes to these topics in a few sentences, what would they be?

China is a massive landmass. There are many different ethnicities. I am Han, normal Chinese. And wealth, the rich-poor divide is large. Again, I am normal, medium. So everyone thinks differently, there are many differences between people. The different ethnic groups may have religions; some are Muslim, Buddhist, you know? At the moment, I think Chinese people have changed from being very mild to more materialistic. More individual; at first Chinese people are very similar to each other, you know? Passive, they accept things, they didn't want to express themselves, what they think. But now people want to, they like to express themselves. Because of the many things which have changed, and girls are more valued. No matter the gender, if you are smart enough, then you can do well. As long as you try hard!

JIANGXI

September 2013, Plymouth, UK

Linda was born in February 1991 and is from Jiangxi province, 'an old and poor province'. She went to school in Jiangxi, and left to study in Beijing, at the Capital Normal University. Her parents both deal in business, working together. They are merchants for kitchen equipment and cooking facilities. She has one older sister, who is two years older, who quit university without completing it. Linda has been in the UK just over a year, and is entering her second year at Plymouth. She studied Financial Service in China, and International Finance in Plymouth for her undergraduate. She is now studying Business Management for her Masters.

My parents want me to study as long as I want, or as long as I can. They have never mentioned marriage. This year is different, as I asked my boyfriend Rex to come and visit. He stayed for one week. I didn't tell my parents he was my boyfriend, only a friend, but they could tell we were in a relationship. I did tell my mum 'I like him, and he likes me' but she told me I should put my studies first and my relationship second. I didn't tell my dad because he is a little bit traditional, and I am just afraid to talk to him about this. Like, he never allowed me back home too late. Ever since I had a mobile phone, since high school, he called me at around 8pm and asked me to start heading home. And at university, he would ring around 9pm to go home. He is changing, but sometimes he keeps calling me if I am not home until late, like 11pm. He would be mad at me. But I know what he likes, so I always go to KFC and buy a coke for him and he calms down. I know his taste, what he likes and what he wants... but about relationships, I don't like talking to him, I'd rather talk to my mum.

How do you think future generations will view Chinese women in the early 21st Century?

I think that when people study my generation they will see that we Chinese women want a more independent life, with a stronger personality. We also have a better relationship with our spouses. When I speak to someone to organise going out for dinner or do something I pay. I don't mind if the boy has money, I prefer to pay for myself. I don't know why, maybe I have been impacted by my parents. They don't like to owe other people. And if I was to end the relationship with the boy I won't owe him anything... I don't like the idea of being controlled, I want my own private space. We are more independent and free. Even my sister, she earns more money than her boyfriend. This is probably because she works for my parents. They don't pay her a direct salary, but they give her a lot of money. Sometimes I think education is quite important, compared between Western people and Chinese people. British people are educated quite well; like, when they buy food in KFC or McDonalds they will say thank you whilst sometimes Chinese don't. I have to say it is the cultural and economic difference. China is too traditional, and China's history is very closed; not much outside influence came to China until recently. That is why we couldn't follow in the footsteps of the West, why we fell behind. Now China has opened and we care more about the education. And the population is another problem. China has the largest population in the world. Too many people… the people in Beijing are educated well because it is the capital and the cultural centre. My country was poor and everything was just like the countryside is now, except Beijing. We still have a big gap… before I went to study in Beijing I was closed-minded. When I went to study I opened my mind, and met well educated people, and sometimes when I go back to my small hometown I hate people who jump queues and do not say thank you. That is my hometown, my home, I must accept this. Rex taught me some things that are bad about mainland people, about what they do in Hong Kong, and I always argue with him about economics and population and culture, anything, when we compare it to Hong Kong.

Many young Chinese women wear clothes that would not be accepted in previous generations. Are these clothes accepted now? If so, why?

I think these small shorts are ok, just not too short! Not so short people can see your bum! These are accepted now because now is the 21st century! Everything has changed, it is different. Even for old people, who cannot accept, HAVE to accept. This is fashion, this is culture now, they can't change anything, and they have to accept it. Let's say… if the designer didn't design and produce those shorts then people wouldn't buy them. But these shorts come out, and people like them, so why not buy some. It is just fashion. Even my mum never wears trousers shorter than to above the knee, always below the knee. But this summer I showed her pictures of Rex's mum, because Rex's mum always wears fairly short trousers. My mum tried to accept, and she even asked if we had any shorts that could fit her, and wanted to have a try, but after she tried she gave up. Maybe because she still can't open her mind, but at least she is trying, she tries now. So, it's fine, I think. Even me, I don't like to wear really little shorts, nothing higher than about half way up the thigh. But this summer I wore new ones, shorter than before... and for the first time I felt uncomfortable. It gave me confidence, and it makes my legs look longer, but sometimes I felt embarrassed and felt people could see my underwear. I would wear my bag low, to cover the tops of my legs, if I felt someone was looking at me. I wear sports shorts underneath to protect myself.

What do you think has changed most since your mother was your age? Do you think anything should change further?

Life has changed a lot since my mum was twenty. Her lifestyle was her workplace and then home, every day. She never went out and had fun. Even now, she never goes out. Home, and workplace. Maybe it's because the business is too busy, and she can't leave, but she has been affected, the way she thinks, is that she can only do this now. For example at night, when she has nothing to do, she still won't come shopping with us. She prefers to stay at home and rest or watch TV and have a shower, then go to sleep. This is her lifestyle now. But twenty years ago, she was a farmer, and worked in fields. She did housework and farming every day. My life is so different. I am well educated, whilst my mum only completed her primary school education. And I have money to spend. She didn't; she had to earn money for the family, and support the family. I needn't. She had to worry about food, the property… so different. So my parents don't want me to have to work hard like them. They want for me, after I graduate, to get a good job and have no need to worry about the salary or baby expenses and have a good man to marry. My parents have known each other since they were children. My father actually already had a fiancé, but gave her up to take my mum. And my mum had a fiancé already too, but the man's family didn't like my mum. That family was rich, so they didn't want a poor woman to enter it. But she met my father, and they met up several times to discuss marriage. My mum's mum doesn't like my father. My father was poor, and my mum's side changed their mind. But my dad still doesn't like them, because they care too much about money,. He still does not like them at all. They care about money too much. My sister had a boy introduced to her by my parents. And this boy's family is quite rich. After they got to know each other better my sister thought that that man was not what she wanted. But my parents felt he was good enough for her, that they were good together, but she didn't want him. It is actually all about the money, my parents care about the money, they don't want my sister to work hard for money in the future. And the boy's parents are really nice, so my parents thought he was a good match. But my sister insisted he didn't match her so my parents gave up. Sometimes my mum still mentions him, even though he is married now… but his wife is not as good as my sister, and our family is better.

Do women have equal opportunities and rights now?

I don't know how girls are treated as a whole… I heard some experiences from my sisters; they are already married but not happy. It's like, the relationship between the mother in law and the daughter in law is a distant one. The relationship is different before marriage, and after marriage it changes. My sisters feel they have an unequal life, and are unhappy. They often meet up and complain about their mothers in law together, and about money, and husbands. Like the husbands don't allow them to do this, do that. They are only allowed produce babies, cook and clean; in Chinese it is *sheng xiao hai de ji qi* which means… that he married her just for a baby, like she is a machine for making babies. One of my sister's best friends, after she got married and had a baby, her husband lost interest. He was always going out with friends, and he had a lot of energy outside but after he came home he was tired and just wanted to sleep and didn't care how the baby was or how his wife was. So my sister's friend is so disappointed about this… she doesn't have a job now, she stays at home every day and looks after the baby, takes care of the baby. In education, I think girls are treated the same. I am not sure about others, but in my class they are treated the same because the teachers are quite nice and never made the girls feel unfairly treated. Perhaps some people felt treated badly, but I never witnessed it.

In the UK and the US having a child out of wedlock is common. What do you think about this?

I don't know if having a father figure is important… But most of my friends my age are already married, and have a baby, and they have to be married. Last year, before I came to the UK, one of my friends spoke to me about him and his girlfriend; and after I came here, I found out his girlfriend got pregnant, and he had to marry her. But his family can't accept this as he is too young, just twenty-three, but later his parents accepted it and the marriage went ahead. Their baby has been born now. Maybe they think the boy must take responsibility, and both sets of parents agreed to the marriage. This sort of thing is common near where I live. Many couples marry early because the girl gets pregnant.

Some people think that dating shows objectify and sexualise women for entertainment. What do you think? How do you think it affects the women (and men) who watch it?

My parents like dating shows, a lot. My father watches these programmes every week, often until very late. He must feel it is interesting, and maybe this is because that they never established a relationship step-by-step, they just got married and had babies. They must find this funny. My uncle loves this show too. My mum said it is because they never got this kind of step-by-step relationship, and that they feel they didn't have a perfect life before. To me, it is just a show for people. I heard that this programme is just an advertisement, promoting itself to make money. It is not real, not what we have

146

seen, it is staged. The women are dressed nice, yes, but it is just a programme! They are on TV, they have to do make up and wear nice dress. Like on the internet you can search 'before makeup, after makeup', ha ha! So it doesn't make them worth less... maybe makeup gives you confidence?

When it comes to dating, what do you feel is important?

The quality I like most in my boyfriend is that he is different, totally different, to most other boys. The other boys I have met aren't as good. Rex is active and good looking. His family matches my family too; not too much money. But I think his parents have much in common with my parents because he told me things about his father, so I think we fit. His family would suit mine. You know, parents are more important in our relationship than many other things. Just like my mum told me, if you want to start a relationship, it is more important that you have a right base, the right foundation, than other things. If parents can solve the problem for you, and can communicate with you well... so parents come first, and location is second. Before I started a relationship with Rex I thought I would not find a man outside my hometown, as I didn't want to live without my parents nearby. But after I met Rex, I told myself maybe I can try to look for a boy outside my hometown, or outside my province. This would be giving myself a chance to live a different life. I would have to change myself.

In a relationship, what is your role? Are you equal?

I don't know about roles really… sometimes it's equal. If I cook, then he washes the dishes. But most of the time I clean the house; usually because I want a clean house, sometimes because I make a mess, but Rex will never clean, even if he makes the mess. I often argue with him over this. But actually this is fine, I just want to get more, more power, to get him to do something I want him to do. But he is a little lazy. At first we said we would split bills and things half and half but sometimes we eat outside and I pay for that, and the next time he will pay for that. But sometimes I ask him 'Do you want me to pay you back? I don't want to owe you' and he will say it is fine, and I will not ask him again. Like today, we were having sushi and he paid. Back at home I asked if he wanted the money and he said no. But sometimes I buy food and things for him, so it is equal. I don't want it to be just him paying. If we were to break up now, we wouldn't argue about the money because we treat each other equally.

If you could sum up Chinese attitudes to these topics in a few sentences, what would they be?

I can't speak about Chinese attitudes, because everything is changing, and keeps changing. Everyone has to accept this. If they can't accept, they are left behind. Like a game. If you can't go on you lose, you are the loser. Chinese attitudes to this will change all the time, because China is changing all the time. In our generation it is much easier to accept new stuff, new things, whilst older people need more time. But this new generation will become old, so things will always change. Like us; most of us come abroad to study and have a different education and different experience and maybe our children will have the same things as we have. I live with my boyfriend, and my parents couldn't have done that.

LIAONING

January, 2014. Birmingham, UK.

Penny is from Fuxin in Liaoning province in the north east of China. She was born in August 1990. Her father is a divisional manger for a very large Chinese telecoms company and her mother is a financial manager in another company. Her mother dropped out of high school, and her father graduated from college; neither went to university, and both are native to Liaoning. She is an only child. She has been in the UK for four months, having graduated Business Economics at the University of Birmingham campus in Ningbo, China. She now studies Investment Analysis. She previously spent two months in the US completing a summer school and she travelled extensively in the US. She has also travelled around parts of China, including Beijing and Hong Kong.

I have a close friend in middle school, and she had several boyfriends when we were schooling. She used to tell me stories about them because we were close. Dramatic things, conflicts and how they got better. For me, it was like watching a Korean drama. I didn't know about other couples, but they were crazy. I wouldn't say it is common to have a boyfriend at that age; my mother disallowed me to have boyfriend until my third year of university, until twenty years of age. And it is not magic, I cannot get a boyfriend immediately, as soon as I turn twenty!

How do you think future generations will view Chinese women in the early 21st Century?

Nowadays, girls my age don't have boyfriends, and don't study that hard. But they are smart, very smart, so they don't need to study hard to get good marks. And, certainly at my university, girls pay a lot of attention to their face, on their makeup, they enjoy their lives. Travelling, eating nice food, always trying to lose weight, ha ha! Some have a very good attitude towards finding a job, but some are lazy. They don't want to bother; they find it takes too much effort, so they will ask their parents for help. Boys do this too, but especially girls. A lot of my friends prefer that, because that kind of job may be easier, less pressure. We call this *guangxi*, having relations. We are much more independent now. Maybe because we only have one child, we are more independent than before. And I think boys are more dependent now, actually.

Many young Chinese women wear clothes that would not be accepted in previous generations. Are these clothes accepted now? If so, why?

This fashion is accepted in well-developed cities; in Southern China it is common, it is acceptable. But only the girls who have a good body [can wear such clothes]. Fat girls would have to lose weight before wearing these clothes. But girls in good shape will feel very confident. But in some less developed places, like my hometown, it is unacceptable. Sometimes, if I wear a shorter skirt, my mum will get angry. She wants me to wear traditional dresses, not far above the knee. More conservative. I think it is accepted in big cities now because they are more modern, and have more foreign influence. People in these cities don't care about each other; I could wear what I want in Shanghai because nobody knows me and nobody cares about other people. But in smaller cities, where people know each other, I couldn't. My mum is traditional, but my father is quite open. When I go to swim, he actually wants me to wear a bikini! When I came to the UK I wanted to take a swimsuit, which I usually wear, but my father said 'No, you are going to the UK! You must wear a bikini!' He feels I am a young woman, and I should feel confident and relaxed.

What do you think has changed most since your mother was your age? Do you think anything should change further?

My mother has four siblings, and she is number three. Her elder brother is disabled. For whatever reason, her mother, my grandmother, died when my mum was in the second year of high school. Due to the circumstances, my mum took the role of my grandmother, and started work. At the age of twenty she had already been working for two years and was saving for the family, to deal with these burdens. That is younger than me! When she was twenty-five she went to an adult college to study a profession. That's her life. She always says that when she met my father she was earning a lot more than him because she had been working seven years longer than him, and was therefore on a higher wage bracket.

Do women have equal opportunities and rights now?

I don't think we have equal opportunities. When I was trying to find a job in banking, I found many places only wanted boys. Because boys are clever; they reflect better than girls. Especially in science or industry. There is still discrimination; my friend comes from Guizhou province and in her area girls must pay a dowry when getting married. Girls are expensive! So they don't want to waste money on her education. I think the wives do most of the cleaning, unless the family is rich and can hire a cleaner. And these tend to be women too…

In the UK and the US having a child out of wedlock is common. What do you think about this? Is it a bad thing, or a good thing, or does it not matter?

My parents can accept single mothers. Last year my mother had an argument with a couple. We were in the supermarket, and we had put our things on the conveyer belt. They were behind us, and thought that we didn't want some of the items. Maybe they were placed apart from the others, I don't know. When we went to pay we found some of our items missing. My mother asked 'Where is the rest of our stuff?' and the boy in the couple said 'I put it away.' My mother asked why, and he said that 'I just put it away, I thought you didn't want it!' and started to get angry. No reason, just got angry. My mother has a bad temper too, but tried not to anger him. I can't remember exactly why they started to fight, but he hit my mum. She hit him back, of course. She is strong. But she is old, over fifty. When he struck my mum the boy's girlfriend moved in front of him and pointed at her stomach and shouted 'Beat here! Beat here! I am pregnant!' Is this common or not, I don't know. I was just so angry. This was shortly after my operation to have my appendix out, so I couldn't help. I was still recovering, and I was so angry! He hit my mum! And I was so angry, so I went to hit him. But I think where I hit him was a good spot; it was weak, behind the ear. I really hurt him. My mum had called the police and they came, but they had connections within the police and blamed the entire incident on me and my mum. My father got really angry about it when he heard. My father has relations with another police station, a bigger one, but my father decided to drop it, because my visa to come here was in process and an incident like that could affect it. The point is, this girl was not married and was pregnant. My mum asked her 'You got pregnant but you are not married? Don't you feel shame? Don't you?' My mum disciplined her, really looked down on her. She also disagrees with sexual behaviour before marriage.

Many women think that dating shows objectify and sexualise women for entertainment. What do you think? How do you think it affects the women (and men) who watch it?

I haven't seen these shows, maybe just once or twice. I don't like them. It is just a show, not real. The girl is not real, the man is not real, they are reading a script. In China, this is unhealthy. Love should be something natural, not rich and pretty. But I believe that the families should be similar. I don't care about these shows. My father sees this and says that the girls are not as pretty as me, ha ah! My father is very cute!

When it comes to dating, what do you feel is important?

The boy needs a good heart. He needs to care about me, care about the family. You know, at my age, because of the one child policy parents like boys. They give lots and lots of love to the boys, and in my opinion these boys are rubbish. Maybe I will find a man who is more mature. I think I would still like a Chinese boy though. I think it matters that we have the ability to communicate; if I am very rich and my family is well educated but his family has a farmer's education we will have totally different lifestyles, which could lead to conflict. This is the cause of many divorces in China. I don't want this. Similar lifestyles would be essential. We need communication between the families, not just us two. Also, because I am a girl, I may go to live with his family. The relationship between the husband's mother and the wife can lead to many issues in China… I don't know about the UK.

In a relationship, what is your role? Are you equal?

It doesn't matter who earns more, I don't care. But if my husband is Chinese, maybe he will care. I will put make up on most days if I have time, but sometimes be freer. If I am married or have a boyfriend, he can't ever see me without make up, right? It takes a lot of time, a lot of money. I would do the cooking and cleaning, I think, but not everything. I would want to share a bit. Cooking and washing can be very tiring.

If you could sum up Chinese attitudes to these topics in a few sentences, what would they be?

I think most Chinese people would really frown on pregnancy before marriage, that it would be a great shame. Some of my friends have boyfriends and will not share anything with you unless you are really close, they really keep it a secret. I personally think the sexy clothing thing is fine, but not in the countryside or small city, or poor city. They are poor, less developed, know nothing about it. But in the big cities it is fine. But if it is too sexy we will discuss it and point and judge. But mostly we don't care. There is a common thought in china that no matter who you are you should study well. Since the one child policy, everyone wants their child to get a good education. They can get a good job, girls and boys. But in some places in the south most girls will get married before university or before Masters, at just twenty, which I think is the [legal age of marriage] in China. In traditional China there were girls, just eight years old, who got married, so the government created a law to stop this sort of thing.

SHANDONG

November, 2013. London, UK

Coco was born in March 1991, and is from Qingdao, Shandong province. Her father is a business man, and her mother is an accountant. She finished her compulsory education in her hometown, and proceeded to do her degree at Shanghai Maritime University. This is her first time to leave China. She enjoys watching films, going to bars with friends and 'anything that doesn't involve studying'.

How do you think future generations will view Chinese women in the early 21st Century?

I think women are treated better now than before. Many women fight for equal rights, you know, we want to work same as men, even though some women are treated differently to men... like in the workplace. Men can get the opportunity for promotion and some women don't get a chance. I don't know history well, but when I was born I was treated really well, because I'm an only child. And in my school girls and boys are treated equally... I don't know what the past was like really. But in the future, I think we will be equal.

Many young Chinese women wear clothes that would not be accepted in previous generations. Are these clothes accepted now? If so, why?

For me, to dress in this new and revealing fashion seems normal, but it can be different. There is a girl on a dating show and in her family her father does not allow her to wear any skirts above the knee, just under the knee. Shoulders and chest must be covered; you can't show yourself to boys. But my parents think it is ok, you can wear whatever you like, just don't dress too sexual, too short. I don't think there was a year when it all changed, or a difference between this year and that year, because China since 1979 has opened its door to the world, and more foreigners come to China. We are more open, open minded. We can speak English; maybe French, and most of the children, including my friends and classmates, go to the UK or Australia to study. We're open minded when we return. We now accept this, when before we didn't. And girls like beautiful things, we just follow fashion. Many of my friends prefer international brands, imported goods.

What do you think has changed most since your mother was your age? Do you think anything should change further?

My mother has told me all about how hard her life was before China opened! She liked to tell me what life was like when she was a girl... she wasn't like me, she was born into a big family. She has three brothers and two sisters. Life was difficult for her, as she was a middle child. And she was born in the countryside, *nong cun*, from another area in Shandong province. She wanted to try and change her life... the only way she could do this was to go to university. She studied hard to go to university, and when she finished she was appointed to

158

a job in Qingdao. I have seen photos of her from this time, and she really covers her body. Her hair is different. You know, there is an interesting thing; my mother gave me a dress to wear, that she bought ten years ago. My friends thought it was so fashionable! It is a long skirt, with unique colours. And it can't be found in the shops! All my friends loved it, thought it was so interesting, ha ha! My mother always said that she is jealous of me, that I have the chance to go abroad and study and make friends, because when my mother was my age she had no money and there was little opportunity for Chinese to go abroad to study. It was so different to now. My friend is studying Accounting and Finance, here in London. In her class of forty, maybe thirty-five, or thirty-eight, are Chinese. Chinese people study how to make money, how to maintain money… always money.

Do women have equal opportunities and rights now?

It depends on the family as to whether or not a girl is treated equally at home. In some places, especially in the countryside, they are treated differently. You know, some poor families don't earn enough each year, and cannot support their daughter to go to high school. They have to save money. The bigger sister will have to go to work so the little brother can save up for university. As I said, it depends on the family; every place has rich people, poor people. In school, in education, we are treated equally. There is no difference. In my school in China most of the girls study better than boys. So it is better to be a girl! But in the workplace I think they are treated differently. When I graduated in Shanghai, earlier this summer, I applied for a summer internship. But some requirements were that they only needed boys, not girls. Things like marketing, where you need to communicate with people, they don't like girls. You need to be able to drink, and girls can't drink. You need to be able to drink with your customers, your clients, and girls can't drink. Families don't like their girls getting drunk, in case they do crazy things, like have sex with guys; this view is common. Chinese girls like foreign guys, you see. When I was in Shanghai I was in a bar, at about 2am, and I saw a foreign guy, a white guy, with two girls, one under each arm, getting into a cab. So... yeah. Many foreigners study in Shanghai, at Fu Dan University. It was full of foreigners; the only Chinese were me and my friend. An old man tried to invite me to dance, I was frightened! He just asked to dance but I ran away.

In the UK and the US having a child out of wedlock is common. What do you think about this?

Why don't men bring up the baby? Why doesn't the mother leave and the father bring up the baby!? For me, I couldn't have a baby without being married. It is important, I think you should commit before having baby. It is a hard life for a woman to bring up a baby alone. You must work for money and take care of the baby; you won't have time to think about anything. Babies are small, and need lots of care, you would end up leaving it with your parents... this is not as common a phenomena in China as in the UK, but the number is increasing. You see these dating shows? Lots of single

160

mothers. It is traditional in China for the mothers to bring up the baby. Mum keeps the baby. I think my parents would not allow me to have a child before getting married. They always tell me not to sleep with a guy until we're married. It's tradition. In ancient times, in old times, you can only have sex with a guy after you have been married, that is normal. But if you have sex with a guy, or have a baby, without being married, even if he is your boyfriend, you could break up easily. I don't know the difference between married and unmarried but my parents really see it... it is just tradition, I don't really know! Other people would think you were a bad girl, and you would find it hard to find another husband. With a baby, it would be very hard to find another man. Some guys think it is ok, as long as there is love, but not all guys think like this. It would be hard, if you were to marry, and have *another* baby, it would be difficult to treat them equally. If I was a parent and my girl had a baby without marriage, other people would look at me and her and wonder how I had educated her... they would think I couldn't bring her up properly.

Some people think that dating shows objectify and sexualise women for entertainment. What do you think? How do you think it affects the women (and men) who watch it?

When I was in university in Shanghai I never watched these shows, as I didn't have time, or a TV... but my parents watched every episode. We think that some girls who appear on these shows do it not just to find a boyfriend or a husband, but to get famous and on TV. That girl who said she would rather cry in a BMW than laugh on a bicycle, she is famous now! She just wants to find a rich guy. Some boys go to this show to try and net their favourite girl. Maybe because she is beautiful, has a good body. And the girl may go with the boy, but straight away, they break up. If you want to take a girl, you must do a lot of work; the boy must try to make himself the ideal man., and after the show the woman finds the man is not perfect! This show is just for entertainment, but some girls do find their Mr Right. In China, many girls cannot find a good boyfriend because they work every day, and know few people, just old friends and colleagues, and don't meet new people often, so it's hard for them to find a boy to love and marry. Dating shows offer a chance to meet guys, to find Mr Right, but the chances are still small. Because it is a show, a lot of it is not real. When you hear the girl ask questions, they are always like 'Why do you do this? Why did you choose this job? How much do you earn?' ha ha! 'Do you have a house, do you have a flat, what do you plan to do, where do you plan to work? If you don't work in the same city as me there is little chance for us'. I think love should be sacrifice. If you find someone you really love you can move and change work to be nearer them. It is not a big issue.

When it comes to dating, what do you feel is important?

For me, there is only one requirement; I'd need to love him. I don't care about money, house… I don't know, I'd just need to see him and think he is really nice… a good personality. Caring, kind, nice, honest. My most recent ex, when we first met we would go to the pub and talk a lot, and I thought he was a really nice guy. I almost fell in love with him, but we had a lot of problems and it did not work. I mean, we met in March and became a couple at the end of April. I had already applied for my UK visa, to study here for a year. He didn't want to lose me for a whole year... we had a lot of differences. At this time, he was working in another city in Shandong. We met in Shanghai, but he is from the same province. He had already graduated, he is older than me. He is 25 now, and I am 22. He used to think I am too childish; he is working now and I am still studying, and I don't appreciate how difficult and mature his life is and I am too much like a child. He is not wealthy; he is well paid, but could never afford a flat in Shanghai.

In a relationship, what is your role? Are you equal?

All boys are different. But most Chinese guys, when you go out, they will pay for you. It is tradition. Some boys think that girls should pay themselves, but some think they themselves should pay for everything, a sort of etiquette. When we were dating we could not cook, we did not have kitchen, so we would go out and have something. He would usually pay, but sometimes I would pay. We were students, we didn't have much; I couldn't ask him to pay all the time! And I couldn't be a housewife. My friend thought that that was what I wanted, and I asked 'If that were so, why would I be here? You do not need to be a post graduate to be a housewife!' My mother and father think I need to earn money; not so much, but enough to support myself, at least. You can't rely on your husband or boyfriend for everything. What if your marriage is not stable, and you break up? If you can get married, you can get divorced. And if you get divorced with no money and no job, life would be very difficult. If you rely purely on him, and you divorce, then it would be hard. This is common, many women in China are housewives, and when they divorce they don't know what to do. And some of them are fifty or forty, they cannot find a job, they have to do little things, earning just 2000 yuan a month, which is not enough to pay rent or support a child. Life would be hard for you. I really think boys and girls should be equal. If boys go to work, then the girl should too. Earn money; support the family, so you don't have to rely on the boy. Some boys feel a lot of pressure; buy a house, buy a flat, buy a car, so much pressure. Work together!

If you could sum up Chinese attitudes to these topics in a few sentences, what would they be?

I think it really depends on different people, as we have different opinions. I have already explained mine… some girls, who are not treated equally, would have different views to me. I am lucky, I am an only child, and my parents really treat me better, and do what they can for me. My old roommate, though, was one of four. The oldest of four. Three girls, and then a boy, and her parents stopped at the boy. It is hard for her. She is the oldest, and when she finishes studying she must got to work and earn money to support her little brother and little sisters. And for girls like this, it is very hard to find a boyfriend or husband. Many boys, particularly nowadays, are from one child families. They would not want to marry her, as she is poor, and they would also

164

have to help her pay the education fees of her younger siblings. Even a boy married to a single child must pay for everything, as he will have to help support her family as well as his. So I think her answers to this would be very different to mine. Because I was born in a very equal environment, a really good environment, so I read about inequality, and hear many stories, but I never experience it. I think things are really good, except when I try and find a job, then I find men and women are different and many jobs do not want women, and I feel angry. Only rubbish jobs hire only women; secretaries and things, or handing out fliers… maybe 200 yuan a day, for six hours or so. I know people who earn 1500 yuan a month, full time. Some others of my friends are very open minded, very open as families. I think education would be the main factor for determining what people think. If your parents are educated and liberal then you can learn and explore, but those from traditional families are narrow minded, and ban you from doing things. You must do things their way, respect them, and not have your own ideas. If you have such parents, narrow minded parents, it is hard to accept differences. *Bao fa hu* are people who become very rich in one night, one transaction. They are still narrow minded and traditional.

SHANGHAI

November, 2013. London, UK.

Clara was born in March 1990 in Shanghai, where she lived until moving to the UK for her Masters. Her mother works for the government, in a Women's Rights department, and her father works for a very well respected Chinese university. She studied at Shanghai Maritime University, and then took part in an exchange and studied for a year at Plymouth University. She is now at the University of Arts London and University of St Martin's. She has previously been to Australia, Thailand and Scandinavia. She studied Graphic Design as a BA, but now studies the creative applications of graphics and art.

How do you think future generations will view Chinese women in the early 21ˢᵗ Century?

In Shanghai and Hong Kong, the girl is powerful, and they can do what they want, but they still have to obey some rules. They cannot sleep with too many guys, as people will think they are a slut. But you can still choose, you and your partner, to make a rule, to be 'friends with benefits' which keeps the sex secret, so people don't think you are a slut. The girls from other places, such as Harbin, are very tough, and people in the far north and far south, are powerful but in different ways. We are powerful in our lives, we tell our husbands

'Do this, do that', but at home, the husbands take back control, and the wife must be obedient. And if they meet with friends, the woman would have to give the man face. I think this is also related to regional habits. In some areas there are different minority groups, each with its own rules. I think people from the northern areas have curious manners and etiquette. They think we, from the south, are savages, and that they had to educate us. In the Qin dynasty they called us, and those in the interior, savages. But now it has changed, we are near ports and can do business easiest. The richest cities, like Shanghai, have large ports.

Many young Chinese women wear clothes that would not be accepted in previous generations. Are these clothes accepted now? If so, why?

Sometimes I would wear small shorts, but when I was slim! Not now, ha ha! Because we don't want to wear clothes like our grandmas! My grandma is a very well educated lady, and is very powerful... although my great grandmother could not even write, she was strict with my grandmother and forced her to study hard, and she was always the top student in the school. She managed everything, she was very well organised. She used to put on lipstick, when she was younger, and she wears pretty clothes, but this is her fashion. Girls in Shanghai keep chasing fashion, keep following fashion. We follow it more than other girls. This fashion is because Deng Xiaoping said we could open our gates, get the information from the foreigners, and learn from that. Did you know, before the Second World War, Shanghai was called the 'Eastern Paris?' We got very fashionable

European designs. They could even wear bikinis at this time! Although only on posters, but still! One of my courses is in advertising, and I have found that Shanghai people use females to make the product sexy, particularly smoking cigarettes. It is about business. We have Topshop, H&M, Zara. It is a retail store, we have them everywhere! Most second line cities now have these stores too, but only Shanghai and Shenzhen have Topshop. They will set up some middle class and luxury brand stores in Beijing or Shanghai as a test zone for sales. And we call the people with money from the north *tu hao*, which means they buy the expensive things and not the right things. I saw a Chinese woman in Selfridges and her accent was northern, making a phone call with her husband and I overheard her saying *ba bao li*, which is how Chinese say Burberry. But, if you have real taste, you would just say 'Burberry'. And she was talking so loud, so proud to be buying luxuries and being rich.

What do you think has changed most since your mother was your age? Do you think anything should change further?

My mother doesn't say about whether a woman's life is easier now, but her personal life… My mother's family used to be poor. Although both my grandparents had good jobs, they were still poor as the government controlled the finances. My mum told me her childhood is not as happy as mine, but it happened in every family, to everyone, rather than just her family. My mum used to wear a skirt, and my dad even bought shorts for her! Because he travelled, and studied in Australia. My grandmother and grandfather did not earn much, but my family knew what to do and what not to do. They had principles, and rules, to try and make a better life. And my father is from closer to the countryside; my mum always jokes my dad is a farmer, a country boy, ha ha! My dad is smart, a hard worker. He raised my mum's social level due to his good job and good relations with high officials. He also used to work in the transportation sector of the government. My maternal grandmother was also poor, but she holds herself with dignity. My grandma still makes fun of my grandpa for being poorer than her, so now my mum says it to my father! She says 'Many boys chased me, and I got you!' It's just that he was brave enough to ask for a date... but he chased her for six years! My dad didn't care, he just cared about her. I think this is permeating from generation to generation, we learn from the one above.

Do women have equal opportunities and rights now?

Women aren't treated equally in the workplace. I asked my father if I could get a job at his university and he said no. He said that they only want men. Women don't become teachers, just positions like Student Support. They have many students there, and it is hard to manage them all. So if you are a lady, it would be difficult to deal with students like this. My mother told me the government would make a statement that they only need men because women give birth and have to take maternity leave, so it's kind of like that. The company and the government will lose out if you are not there to work and yet get paid still. Companies don't want to pay for this. In the home I think women get more rights than men! My mum cleans and washes and sometimes cooks, but my dad can cook better... most of the Shanghainese men will work and then go food shopping after. When they get home they cook and wash and do the housework. I think men do over half the housework... and the women go shopping. Studying, in education establishments, it is equal. We work together as a team. But sometimes a boy will do more; if we have heavy books, a boy will carry them for us. Girls get the same support, more if they are pretty! In the street, in daily life, women are treated well. Men always carry the bags, or luggage. The boys I know, every time we go out they hold the doors or walk me home. Some even pull the chair out for me.

In the UK and the US having a child out of wedlock is common. What do you think about this?

For me, I would must be married before having a baby. But I don't want to become a mum at all. I don't think my parents would allow me to do this, my dad doesn't even know I have had sex. If he knew, I think he would be very disappointed. You know my mum and my dad knew each other for ages? They never had sex! And I wouldn't want to have a baby to be without having a husband. People will say I am a slut, and this will affect the baby. They would ask the child 'Where is your dad? Where is your dad?' because, you know, children can be very childish. They don't know what they should really say, what is rude, they will just make fun of him, and laugh at him. If I had a baby with a man without being married, the rumours would be very horrible, people would judge me and be cruel, mean… I used to be close with my dad, and I felt he gave me too much pressure. When he went to America for six months I was so happy, but my mum cried so much… I couldn't understand why. I was about ten, or twelve I think. I thought that I wouldn't be forced to do homework! My mum became very anxious and nervous though, and I found that hard to deal with. This is my experience of living without a man, without a father/husband.

Some people think that dating shows objectify and sexualise women for entertainment. What do you think? How do you think it affects the women (and men) who watch it?

My mother said you shouldn't wear make up to look sexy, but to show respect; to look your best for others, it is polite to others. When I go on a date I must wear make-up, but just day to day is not so important. My mum told me a phrase saying not to rely on your partner; lean too much, and you will slip. Women should earn their own money and support themselves. Not be rich, but retain dignity and be responsible for themselves. Self-reliant. It is very common for women to chase rich guys, but I wouldn't mind if my husband is rich or not. He just has to be interesting and fit in with my way of thinking. I think girls on these shows are so stupid, even more stupid than the men! I don't watch it, but when I was last in Shanghai I was really bored so I had a look, just for five minutes, and I saw their age. Some are just twenty-two or twenty-three, and they are on television, trying to find a boy! At my age! At my age, they are supposed to be learning! At university, and they

171

will meet boys there. I think women on these shows should be like thirty or forty, not twenty! If I took part in this sort of show my father would slap me for losing face. It's so fake! One of my friends was in the broadcasting company said it is all fake, they have a script to follow. I saw the British dating shows, and they are quite funny. In the Chinese ones, they look like they need to find a boyfriend. But in the British one they just want to have sex, not caring about later life, the body is most important to them.

When it comes to dating, what do you feel is important?

He has to respect me enough, be polite, and for the first dates he can't be late and must be well presented, well dressed. And quiet, not too loud. Education is important, money not so much. I am not poor, I don't need to use his money to succeed. But he needs to be knowledgeable. My ideal boyfriend should know many things, and be able to guide me when I am confused. Rather than asking what clothes he should wear! He doesn't have to be very handsome, just not make me feel sick, that is enough. Because if a boy looks really bad, I wouldn't wish to touch him… and tidy! He must be clean and hygienic and look tidy. He must wash and have clean hair, these things.

In a relationship, what is your role? Are you equal?

In the beginning, I would follow him. In the first three months I would be a 'hello kitty', but after that I would be tough, tough, tough. Because to start with, I would

172

still be interested in him and things would be new. I really find that star signs are accurate, and my sign says I find it hard to maintain relationships… I am very weird; I chased him [her ex-boyfriend] for a whole year, but when I finally got him, we lasted just eight months. I just lost interest. I reach a plateau quickly, and grew bored, and that effects the communication. Once I reach this stage then it becomes very hard to go back to how things were. If he insists that he pays then that is fine, or if we go half-half that is fine too. I would be happy to earn more than him, because my mother use to earn more than my father; the government has upped tutors' salaries. My grandma also earned more than my grandfather. If you earn more than your partner, it is fine, I can be myself, and he would have to listen to me! Just be myself, and maintain my level of beauty. If I put makeup on every now and again, for special occasions, he will look and go 'Wow, you look good' and he would be proud. But not every day, I would spend so long putting it on and taking it off. My ex-boyfriend would always wash his hair, even if it made us late. We had an argument once because we were so late for meeting friends for dinner. I left, and he still stayed behind and washed his hair!

If you could sum up Chinese attitudes to these topics in a few sentences, what would they be?

I think well educated women will be tougher, because they have been pressed down for so long, and now we can stand up. We will fight for it. We are now equal with men; we can get what they can get. And we want to be better! Women used to wear tiny shoes, and have bound feet, and I saw these shoes in a museum in Australia. I was so shocked! My mum told me they were shoes for Chinese women, I couldn't believe it! I feel sorry for girls who have a low family status, and I really want to help them. But they don't think this is a problem. They accept that their brother will get more food and a better life than them. Last summer I went to a salon to have my hair done and the girl looked the same age as me so I asked her for her age, and she said she was only eighteen or seventeen. I told her 'You can't work!' but she told me she needed to earn money for her brother, that he needed to go to university. I told her 'You also need to go to school. If you can't afford the fee, you can do a part time job or get a loan from the government' but she said 'No, my parents prefer my brother to go to university, to get the education'. This was in Shanghai, but she was from the interior. Why do some parents make this kind of decision? I know it's hard but as parents you have to try to send both your children to university. At that moment I really felt shocked... we are all children of parents, we should be treated the same. I heard that people in the south, Cantonese people, beat their wives. That is awful.

SHANXI

November, 2013. Portsmouth, UK.

Tracey is from Taiyuan, a city in Shanxi province, and is in her early twenties. She is studying her Masters in Business Management in the University of Portsmouth. She has been her three years, having completed her undergraduate in International Business Communication in Portsmouth also. She studied in her hometown before coming to the UK, as well as spending two years in Beijing. She has travelled widely, including countries such as Spain, Germany, France, Turkey, Holland, Ireland and Wales. Her mother is a housewife; she previously worked in a factory but has since retired and stays at home. Her father works in business, dealing with coal as an industrial fuel. She enjoys sports, and actually teaches street dance in the university society, having obtained her level one UK Sports Teacher Certificate, and teaches young children in local schools. She also enjoys swimming, and has done so for many years.

How do you think future generations will view Chinese women in the early 21st Century?

Although I was born in the last century, I was raised in this one. But I know about life back then from my grandma, who was about then. She says Chinese women have many more rights now than in the old days. The most important change is that women can go and work. This is quite a big change. Women can go to work, so they have their own money, and they can buy things themselves. They do not have to wait for the man [for money or permission], they can make their own decisions. In the old days, this could not happen. Chinese men, if their wife went out to work, would think their wife is breaking the rules. I think this is good for women; they have much more choice. In my mum's generation, very few people got divorced. But now, many more people divorce, they have more choice.

Many young Chinese women wear clothes that would not be accepted in previous generations. Are these clothes accepted now? If so, why?

We wear these clothes because we are open now, open to the West, to the world. In the old days, we have no trade, no economic system. Well, when I say no, I mean very limited. Some tea, some fruit, but now we trade a lot, a lot of material, many different things, and we learn from the western countries, and we also learn their culture. It is easy to get a ticket to go to France or Milan to see the fashion shows. This couldn't even be imagined in the old days. People do these things now and follow fashion; they know what fashion means. It is learnt through social traits. When you have more money you will think about what t-shirts you can buy, what sort of skirts you can buy. When you have money you want to buy more. I think the clothes now reveal more because, as I said, it is a social trait; it is fashion. But my grandma certainly doesn't accept it! Because they think that if lots of men can see your body they will want to touch you. My grandmother says if you dress like this you are very attractive to men in the street and on the bus, they may want to touch you. That is why they changed the film Titanic; it is different in the east and the west. They cut the part showing the sex. They are worried that in the 3D version people will try and touch the screen, ha ha!

What do you think has changed most since your mother was your age? Do you think anything should change further?

My mother, this summer, came to see me to celebrate my graduation and travel around the UK a bit. We went to the high street, where there is a shop which sells sexy underwear, and there is also a place which sells women's toys, and I picked one up to show my mum. My mum asked 'What's this?' and I told her 'It is for the woman's pussy' and she was so shocked! She said 'Oh, my little girl, when I was your age I can't even say this word, and I had never seen these things!' but now you can buy it and take it home, maybe share the experience with your friends on facebook. So, yeah, this is very different. In China you cannot see these from the street, but in first line cities like Beijing and Shanghai, they are more open and have a GDP higher than a second line or third line city, and they have these shops. We are influenced by Western culture. But we just go in the entrance and laugh and leave, we do not go in or buy anything. Maybe just go in and say 'Oh, I cannot look at these anymore!' and leave. But British people go in. Women my mother's age people care about their bodies; my mother's first time was with my dad, when they got married, but now people can sleep with everybody before they get married, even in China.

Do women have equal opportunities and rights now?

When I was in school in China there is the one child policy. I knew that a lot of undeveloped people wanted a boy, a son. If they have a girl they will kill the girl and keep trying until they have a boy. Yes, kill. In my class, the number of boys is always higher than girls. Maybe a 60:40 ratio of boys to girls. And when they grow up it will be very hard for them to find girlfriends. And the girls will have more choice of men. So I think in the future women will have more choice to choose men, ha ha! In regards to housework and these things, it is different in different places. Different places have different rules. In some places, some people are happy for their wives to go outside and get skills and knowledge from a company, and are happy to share her experience when she comes back. It makes for good communication. If your wife doesn't go out, there is not much for you to talk about. But in some places men have the responsibility for the whole family, and women do not go outside. They don't have a job. So it depends on the different places. But I'd prefer for women to be able to go outside to work. It is our right. We should have the same opportunities as men. Learn the same knowledge and have the same resources; why should we just stay at home? It is a terrible thing. When I was in school, I thought that women could not do well in exams, but now I know we actually do better than men, and pay more attention to our coursework. We get better grades. You can see, in lots of countries, even the US and UK, after twenty years, how many men and how many women are still working? Men, maybe 90% and women, maybe 30%. Because women must go off and have a baby, they have to give up their job if they have a family. So… actually, every woman in the world has two jobs; their outside job, that is, their paid job, and then they have their family job, their mothering job. So sometimes they have to work so hard, as if they have two jobs. A lot of people do not respect women, look down on women.

In the UK and the US having a child out of wedlock is common. What do you think about this?

I see in the street a lot of women who have babies in pushchairs but no ring on their finger. So I asked my teacher why this is so, and he said maybe they have a boyfriend but never married. I think this is a personal choice. It is nothing like 'You must marry first, and only then have a baby' but I think that this man should take responsibility for this baby and his girlfriend and get married… this is the traditional way that I think. We believe the temple has some rules about marriage and children. In China, the truth is, people have to marry and then have children. If they have a child outside of wedlock, then the girl will try really hard to get the boyfriend to marry her. The girl, and her family, will want marriage. Because in China there are many legal aspects. When the child wants to go to school, and get an ID card, they must have a father, a registered father.

They must be married; then the child can have an ID. Without an ID they cannot go to school. It is difficult.

Many women think that dating shows objectify and sexualise women for entertainment. What do you think? How do you think it affects the women (and men) who watch it?

I think these shows are just for entertainment, and they want to get more viewers and ratings for their show. I certainly do not agree with judging someone just on their appearance. Appearances are nothing; the beauty outside, the beauty inside. But if you have beauty inside and not outside, it would be hard for women to find Mr Right. But to use TV, this is not a good idea. If you can spend time standing on a stage, think about how much time you could spend finding a truly good boyfriend. Just wearing makeup and standing on a stage, rather than having a coffee or a holiday with a boyfriend is stupid, it is not true love. I think this show displays social problems, like women who just chase money. Because they think... basically, China's economy has moved very fast, and in the last ten years, it has moved crazy fast. But this has two sides. If the economy grows too fast, people will ignore little things. They ignore how to be happy with just the simple things, and how to make other people happy. They forget this, and just want money, men who have money. But if he has enough money for you, he also has money he can spend on another girl. You will not be the only one in his life, not special. What is the meaning of love there? There is no love, you only have money. I think Chinese girls should stand back and look around, and live by themselves, not just follow GDP. GDP is actually nothing… we waste and destroy a lot of natural things, and cause problems like environmental pollution, air pollution, to chase the GDP. I came here to learn knowledge, to learn the truth. To learn these things. Every time I see the newspapers it is about China's air pollution. I had lived in Beijing for two years, and I was there for the Olympics. In my memory, the sky was blue, not much pollution. But now the newspapers say there are many problems.

When it comes to dating, what do you feel is important?

I first thing I will see is his face. What he looks like, how much he talks. But these do not differ much between people. I would have to look deeply before I chose him as a boyfriend. I would have to consider his personality, and judge whether he is a playboy who will just play with me or if he would take responsibility. This would mean we would be friends, and then we could date, and then I would get to know his family, his job, his personal goals, and really get to know him. And if he truly loves me, he would share these things with me. And the same with me, if I really love him I would share everything with him, and have no secrets from him. After all those things, money would be the most important factor. Because I am not from a very rich family, my family is just normal, and I know of the lives of poor people from when I watch TV… I am a princess in the eyes of my mum and dad, I do not want my life to become one of poverty. If I found a very poor boy, with nothing, no goals, why should I marry him? It would be a difficult choice. My mother told me the only reason I should accept a boy is because he loves me more than I love him. That is what I would look for.

In a relationship, what is your role? Are you equal?

I refer to live in an equal way... separate. I pay my bills, you pay your bills. But if we are together, one day he can pay my bill and then next day I can pay his bill. I like doing things this way. I have my skills, I have my power. Why should I wait for a boy to send me his money? I can do these things by myself, and I can earn money by myself. So I do not want to get something from him, not this 'old fashioned' way. The same at home, we can have a plan. This week, you do some housework, cleaning, washing, next week, I will. Take turns, equally. This way, if you travel I will do more, and when I travel you can do more. So, I prefer this equal way. If you are married already, and the man pays your bill, it is ok. If you haven't married, just boyfriend and girlfriend, you should not let your boyfriend do this. A lot of my friends are students, and have no income. Boys and girls, both have no income. My mum pays my bill, and the boy's mum pays the boy's bill. It is not personal money, but from the family. It would mean for my mum to allow his mum to pay for me... just pay your own bill! If you are and your partner are married, you are a new family. It is your money, you pay for yourselves. But if your money comes from your dad, it is ridiculous.

If you could sum up Chinese attitudes to these topics in a few sentences, what would they be?

I'm not good at summaries, ha ha! I think that the Chinese women have more rights now, when compared to the old days. Some still think women are lower than men. Some cultures, in the countryside, the poorer areas, think this. They think women my satisfy their husbands and mothers and do lots of housework. They must give birth to a boy, and do everything! But in the city women have more choices, more rights, they can choose their boyfriends. My friend changes her boyfriend every week, ha ha! She's in Beijing, and she is a manger for a company. She's not a slut, but she is charge of her life and her body. Do you know what I mean? In the old days she would be called a *po xie*, or party girl, but now she thinks it is ok.

SICHUAN

January, 2014. Birmingham, UK

Lily is from Mi Yang town in Sichuan province, central China and was born August 1989. She has been in the UK for five months at the time of the interview, and studies Marketing Management at Aston University in Birmingham. She has travelled before to the US, when she was fifteen, and she has also been to UK before; she visited the UK for the first time when she was twenty-one. She has also covered much of South East Asia. She has also travelled a lot of China internally. She has an older sister, who is one and half years older. Her parents had to pay for Lily to study abroad, but due to guangxi they weren't hit as hard as a normal family; she claims her family knew someone in the correct department. Her sister also went to university and now works for a Chinese firm in China, having studied in Manchester. She has been working for three years. The company deals in real estate and amenities. Her father deals in real estate and development and her mother is an engineer.

How do you think future generations will view Chinese women in the early 21st Century?

In world standards, the time difference between now and 1949 is not much. So people in the future who may study China will think that we have gained a lot and have improved a lot since 1949, and since Mao's time. I think they will feel that rights for women are increasing, but maybe not as rapidly as it will in 100 years from now. But it is improving, it is good. It is much better to be born now than before. For my parents, their generation… I mean, most families who are wealthy now had many opportunities which we may not have now. They could make a lot of money even if they were not well educated. But for us, we have a higher level of education, although we may not get as good a job. My parents were able to earn a lot of money without having to go to university. I am lucky, my family has succeeded. I think, for girls though, it is easier to get a job for my generation than my mother's. When my mother was young maybe it wasn't very easy for her to get a job, but for me it is much easier.

Many young Chinese women wear clothes that would not be accepted in previous generations. Are these clothes accepted now? If so, why?

I think because Chinese people are influenced by Western styles and culture, and we can use the internet to see a lot of pictures to see what Western people are doing. We also have many corporations and companies which deal with the West. People become more open in their mind. People are wealthy now, more than our parents, so they have money to buy clothes and luxuries. Our retail sector is now well developed, girls want to buy more clothes and leggings and things. I think it is because people are more open minded. But it isn't accepted by everyone. I think my parents, or teachers, or people working in the government, they wouldn't accept their daughters wearing clothes too hot, or too sexy. My parents do business, and I'm not sure how they feel… but the former [generation], their parents wouldn't accept. My parents are very good parents, they support me and my sister, as long as we maintain their principles. I have tattoos on my body, very little ones; I have just had a new one done recently. At first I told my mum I have a huge dragon on my back, so when I showed her it was just a really little star, she wasn't very angry! She just accepted it, but when my father saw it he asked if it was fake. I smiled and didn't respond. He doesn't like me wearing short clothes… they are good parents. They won't force me to remove them, or to do things I don't wish to do.

What do you think has changed most since your mother was your age? Do you think anything should change further?

My mum was the youngest in her family; she has five older brothers and sisters, and my grandmother really didn't like girls. She really didn't like my mother. They were from the country, you see. She often left the children alone (my grandfather died due to health issues, maybe from drink, when my mother was very small) and when my mother wanted to go to school my grandmother refused to pay the fees. I think just five pence for the fees for the term. But my uncle, who was working in the town, paid for her education. And it turned out she is the clever one in the family. But she only has junior school education. My father also only studied in junior school. My mother's life was tough as a child, but after she met my father his family paid for her to take accounting lessons, and learn from my father's business. Back then they didn't bother to invest in girls. During new years our parents give us money in red envelopes; my grandmother always gave less to my mother, and to the other girls, than the boys. The same thing happened with meat. But my father's parents have just one boy, and three girls. They treated the kids equally… but not my mother's family. Both are from the country.

Do women have equal opportunities and rights now?

I'm not sure about the whole market… I have been to companies to work in sales, and they don't judge on age, just outlook and background, not gender. Speaking and communication skills are highly valued. They don't judge on gender. I don't know about other companies. Maybe for different kinds of jobs they may like males better than females, but I don't have experience of this. At school, we are treated the same. Actually, I think teachers like girls better, because boys can be naughty and don't always concentrate on their studies. And girls do much better than boys in terms of grades. And girls listen to the teacher, whilst boys muck about.

In the UK and the US having a child out of wedlock is common. What do you think about this?

I have friends who got married during their pregnancy, and I mean it is obvious to see the bump when she is wearing her wedding dress, and my mother wouldn't approve. Even though they are getting married, she still got pregnant before. If they don't get married and have a baby it would be even worse. This kind of issue is not very common in China, and is not good in our parents' minds. I can't accept it, and I hope it would never happen to me. I think it isn't good. But you have an abortion, though that isn't good either, so it is very complicated. Surgery can mean you can't have children in the future, but if you have the child without a husband it would be very hard to find a new boyfriend or partner.

Some people think that dating shows objectify and sexualise women for entertainment. What do you think? How do you think it affects the women (and men) who watch it?

I think that dating shows can show good and bad sides to people. It depends on the girls; some girls would say they have quite high expectations regarding boys. But some are really independent, and they can look after themselves, they don't need a man to buy them luxury things and they are very happy and comfortable being single; they may have very high standards. For these kinds of girls, the information they give the audience may be that they're very materialistic, but actually I don't think so, because they have the ability to get these things themselves. And for the hosts who give advice, they really give very good advice, but they can be very mean to the male guests. And the presenters can make conclusions, to clarify bits for the audience, explain it. As a woman, I find it really very entertaining. I really like those hosts which give advice. But I think some of the girls can be so mean to the guest; there is no reason for them to say such mean words!

When it comes to dating, what do you feel is important?

Humour, and generosity, are the most important things a boy must have. If a boy is very mean, that isn't good... I don't need him to be wealthy, but not be tight with his money. Not just with me, but in his life. And humour will make our relationship more interesting. Not too ugly, not too fat, not too short, even though I am short, ha ha! If tall boys don't mind my height, then a tall boy would be good! And well dressed, well presented. And short hair!

In a relationship, what is your role? Are you equal?

Most of the boys I have dated were at junior and senior school, and we didn't have too much to worry about; no chores. Just have fun together, eat together, no responsibilities. If I had enough money I would hire someone to clean; if I didn't, we would share, I definitely wouldn't do these things alone. Payment for meals and things depends on our stage of dating; if we have just met, a few weeks or a few months, then it would be better for him to pay the bills, but I wouldn't mind paying. But after we have a mature relationship, we should deal with money in a fairer way. He needs to pay first to build a good impression; as I said, I like generous boys. And if he is generous here, I would see different aspects and what sort of person he is. If he is mean to me, then he won't be generous to his friends or

189

other people. Likewise, we should treat our friends and they will treat us back.

If you could sum up Chinese attitudes to these topics in a few sentences, what would they be?

For me, I think it is a good thing for girls to have more rights, and more opportunities to get into jobs. Males are no longer the most important in society; we don't need to live under them anymore. Maybe for my generation, most girls would agree. But maybe my mother or grandmother, when we were talking about dresses and things, they may think girls are too materialistic. But my generation feels independent, and that we don't need to rely on others. But many others may like to rely on men, and stay at home as a housewife. But for most girls we must try to raise our social standing to that of men.

December, 2013. Portsmouth, UK

Leanna was born in February 1993 in Sichuan province, in the south of China, and has been in the UK just three months at the time of the interview. Before she came here, she studied at Shanghai Maritime University in Shanghai. She lives with her parents in Sichuan, and is an only child. Her mother is an English teacher at a middle school, whilst her father is an official for a national company. Both her parents are native to Sichuan. In Shanghai she studied English, specialising in shipping terminology. In Portsmouth, she studies International Trade and Business Communications.

My family is kind of interesting. Usually, in Chinese families, the father will be the bread winner, but in my family my mum earns more than my dad, as a teacher. When I was a child, every time I wanted to buy something I would go directly to my mum, to ask her to buy it for me. And she keeps making jokes saying that I should change my family name to hers [Chinese children take their father's family name, whilst the mother keeps hers], *since she has say over most of things. So the thing in my family is that my mum is really strong minded, and takes charge of most things in ten house, and although my dad is really kind and gentle, when big problems arise he would take ideas from my mum. And my mum will always say 'Ok, I will take care of it'. Things like money or whatever. Sometimes our relatives want to borrow money, or we need to borrow from them. My dad is really shy, and doesn't know what to say, but my mum will always take care of it. Another thing is that we went out to dinner, many times, my mother was always the one to pay, and she liked it! I*

191

can see from her face, she likes to pay! And sometimes my dad pulls out his wallet, and can see the bill, but my mum always insists that she pays. I think she must earn a lot more, as on top of her salary she can earn extra by being a private tutor. And she is really good at her job; every exam period her classes get the highest scores. So she always has the idea... many times she told me 'You have to be strong, you have to be economically independent'. I think she inherited that mind-set from her mother. They both think that even when you are married you must be strong; you must be the one to pay for your own stuff. Even if you don't have to; for example, maybe if you need to buy an expensive suit, you shouldn't beg your husband like other women do, you should pay for that yourself. So I think they represent these independent women in China, the tough women. I have friends, class mates, whose mums are typical housewives. So when we talk about these things they find my family weird. This is not common in China, as in most families the dad will earn more. And most people have this idea in their head that men HAVE to be better than women, and that men have to be the stronger one, to provide, but for my family it is the opposite. Sometimes I felt sad that my family was different from my friend's but my mother told me as long as we are working as a family, it doesn't matter. I think maybe I will become like my mum, even though I don't want to, ha ha ha!

How do you think future generations will view Chinese women in the early 21st Century?

I think that ever since Deng Xiaoping became the new leader, everything changed. It was another cultural revolution! Now, I can feel women become really independent. I can feel it. Before this new revolution, people would think that women could not wear something too short, reveal yourself too much, even be too strong at work. I think this is because we have been affected by the western culture, and women are beginning to think 'we can'. Dresses are becoming shorter and shorter, I don't think they can become any shorter! I think girls are getting more attention from society. I mean, now there are many more boys than girls in China, and this has caused a problem. You know, girls have more value now. Some women are still unmarried though. There is a saying; if a woman is independent and single at thirty, people would worry about her. But people outside the family will think she is too good, too well educated. That she would say 'That man, he can't match me'. But when a boy is still not married at thirty, people will think 'You are a loser. You are not good enough.' People will think that! That is why I say girls have a higher value. If a boy wants to marry a girl, the family will want to know that the boy is good enough, and can afford a good life for her... even if the girl is not very good. That's the thing. He must have a car, a good job. People became realistic. The woman must check that they can afford a flat, and you know in Shanghai is VERY expensive. Women are now more proud of themselves. And lesbians, the number of lesbians is rising, I know it. They can be more open, and proud, and more willing to expose themselves as lesbian. But in the past people would think that this shouldn't be done, and girls must behave themselves and be elegant. But now you can see many girls who are confident, lesbian or not. I don't know what the future will be like, but I think it will be more and more empowering for women. If there remain less women than men, which I think there will, they will become valued more and more.

Many young Chinese women wear clothes that would not be accepted in previous generations. Are they now? If so, why?

I will say that this is people being affected by western cultures. Western TV shows are very popular in China. Things like Gossip Girl, Friends... from these TV shows people began to get to watch real life in western culture. What people wear, how they live, their lifestyle, and Chinese people thought 'How can I be like this?' There are many foreign brands now entering the Chinese market. We produce western style clothes and people want to look like western people. They dye their hair; I know a Chinese girl here, who obviously has black hair, and one day she was in front of me but I didn't recognise her, I thought she was British, because she dyed her hair blonde! I thought she was British, the colour was really good, until she turned around. I said 'Oh my god, it's you!' and she smiled and said 'I've dyed my hair, you know' She looks Korean now, ha ha! So strange to have blonde hair and a typical Chinese face. Girls are affected by that, we are attracted to western cultures and fashion. I thought when I first arrived here that people wear very little. Not just in the summer, but the winter too! I always thought 'Won't you feel the cold!?' and this is another reason. Chinese come here and wear a lot and see British people wearing very little. And girls want to be like this. Sometimes, you can't feel pretty when you are all covered-up, and I think this is due to western culture. I think that not everyone in

China accepts this, but some of them certainly do. According to my observations, I think there are two types of people in this concern, two classes of youthful people. The first are those who are affected by Western culture. They wear American clothes, watch American shows, and want to travel abroad to America and Europe and maybe study there. And the other group is affected by Korean culture, or Japanese. Not all of the Chinese teenagers hate Japan; some do, but some really like them, and many girls watch Korean shows and admire the actors. Things like KPOP. All those left, unaffected by either, are traditional, affected by their parents. I have a friend, a boy, who is a very traditional Chinese. You can't take him into a bar for more than two minutes before he says 'Argh! It's too loud!' and I say 'Well, yes, this is a bar, it is like this!' He does drink, he just thinks it's too loud. He always says it is better in China, that we have better things. The saying is that if you want to beat someone, you must learn their ways. It comes from the old saying about learning from the Western 'barbarians' in order to beat them. We asked him why, if he thinks that China is so great, did he come to the West, and he just replied 'You have to learn from your enemies in order to beat them'. We are friends from China, we studied at university together. So I think he is affected by his parents' culture.

What do you think has changed most since your mother was your age? Do you think anything should change further?

I think the thing that has changed most is the attitude towards marriage. I'm my mum's age, in the 80s, people

195

were still closed minded. They thought that women should marry the first man they date; my mum has only dated one man in her life, and that is my dad. And many parents are like that. They would say 'Well, I know a boy, I think he would suit you', and they would arrange a meeting and the boy and girl would be expected to get married. But now, their attitude has changed a lot. We don't just have playboys, we have party girls too! I know girls like this from my university. They are very good looking, and they keep changing their boyfriends, keep changing. And they act like playboys in their attitudes to dating. They just want to marry a man who is rich. They just want to enjoy being popular, being chased by men, having men begging to be with them... they are more open to sex before marriage. In the old times, girls would marry the first man they dated, whilst now girls would not even marry the first man they sleep with! So, yeah, the change in attitudes is the biggest. And also the attitudes towards children. In the past, when Mao was leader in the 1950s, when China was young, he wanted to encourage people to have many babies to make China strong. That is why we have such a large population, which is now actually causing problems... Women were even given a medal if they had ten kids, and would be called a hero mums! But I know some women now, who are older than me, maybe thirty, and when you ask them if they are going to have a baby they say 'Oh, I don't know, maybe.' They are focussing on their job, they don't want to lose their position. You are in competition with other people in the workplace, and you would need to ask for a really long period of leave if you wanted to have a baby. This long period of time is when you would lose your position. Because of this, many women who work in international companies will not do have a child. Having kids is not their first priority. In my mum's time women would have the baby the first year after being married, maybe even earlier, but now women don't choose to do this.

Do women have equal opportunities and rights now?

It is hard to use the word 'equal'... I remember my philosophy teacher taught me 'If you are not given special rights, there is no room for equality'; only when women and children are given specials rights are we treated equally. But some people take it literally and think that to be equal means to be treated the same. I think things are getting better. I don't hear much news about women being treated badly by their company anymore. But I remember a few years ago we heard this story on the news that a woman got an interview for a company, and the first question was 'Are you married?' as they were worried that if she was married she may want to have a baby and take time off work. Now, you don't hear much news like this, so I think things are getting better. But we still have a long way to go until things are really equal. Because some companies, when there is a vacancy, will choose the man first, but it is getting better. I think household status is a regional thing... In Shanghai, some men are really good at home keeping and such things, and we say that they have 'soft ears'. I know that some boys are good at cooking, and they share these tasks with their partners, whilst in places in the north east of China I was told that the boys there are really tough, 'I am the man of the house, and the woman has to do her job, which is cooking and cleaning', that sort of thing. The thing is, it is a problem which varies from province to province. In my house, it is my mum which does the most cleaning and cooking, and my dad does nothing! He doesn't win most of the bread, and he doesn't take care of the home either; but my mum really enjoys it! She really enjoys cooking! My dad would just relax on his own. Family friends always say he is so lucky to find a girl like my mum. In some families women still have traditional roles, and have to do these tasks. But nowadays, especially young couples, like my aunt and uncle, cannot do any of this house-related stuff, they both depend on my grandparents. Some young couples have this issue. They will live with, and depend on, their parents for the housecleaning and to bring in food and wealth. It is really strange, but ever since China got the one child policy, it means that the child becomes the most valuable treasure in the house. Regardless of whether it is a boy or girl. In rural areas, they will think boys are of a higher value, because girls have to marry and leave the family, whilst the boy will stay with you and keep the name, and you will have grandchildren in your name. But there is a saying if your daughter marries away; 'Spilling water out the cup'. You can't get it back, it is wasted. But now in the big cities both sexes are the most valuable treasures. They are relied on to provide a good life for the family. They must both study very hard, to bring benefits to the family. We ignore things like common sense, we just teach them to study hard and get good grades. They have this ridiculous idea that if you are rich, everything can be solved! Like, 'Although my son cannot cook, if he is rich and has a good job he can hire someone to cook and it won't matter'. Some young couples are like this. A few days ago I read in the newspaper that some young couple spends thousands of yuan a month on hiring someone to clean their house and eating out every single day. And after some time, the man tried to divorce the woman because he thought she was useless. But his wife said that he was useless too, and finally it had to be settled to the court. He [the judge] made them, demanded, that they learnt to cook and clean. I mean, this actually went to court! And the judge must have thought it was ridiculous. He demanded they try again, another way.

In the UK and the US having a child out of wedlock is common. What do you think about this?

Here's a funny story; I was hanging out with my flatmates and talking about things, and one of them [a British] said she was thinking about having a baby, as it is so cute. She began to make jokes that she could marry a flatmate and move in with him, and it moved on to asking whether I would have a baby with that boy, if I was really desperate to have a child... This was all joking, ok? I said I wouldn't, as it would be too hard to raise a baby on my own, and my flatmate said 'No, it isn't. My mother raised me on her own.' I wanted to say that I was sorry, I don't know, and she said that it was really common here, and that her dad just shows up whenever he wants. That was my first experience of single parents in the UK. I think that I accepted it, but in my point of view it would be a little bit difficult, as you would have to raise the family on your own. I mean, women can earn enough now, but still... I think the child wouldn't be loved completely. I mean, if you have a boy, the mum can earn enough to give him everything, but you will never be able to have some to play football with him. Or teach him how to treat his girlfriend. The father has a role to play. The same if a dad is raising a daughter alone, you would need a mother figure. My attitude towards this is accepting, but it is not for me. In China, I would say this is becoming accepted, but only by the law. People will still say things. If you are a young women, and you suddenly showed up on your own with a child, people will begin to ask 'Did you get divorced, or just have a boyfriend who doesn't want to pay and take responsibility?' There is a really good [Chinese] friend of mine, who was raised by her mother; her parents got divorced when she was only five or six years old. She turned out very well, but my mum would talk with me about how it is not easy to raise a child in China. When her mum and dad were getting divorced, they signed an agreement that the dad would leave them the house and was exempt from having to pay the monthly payment. I know that her mum and her father share the tuition fees, half and half, and people need to be open minded. So many people are getting divorced. In ancient China men were allowed to have as many wives as they wanted, and he only needed to write a statement saying 'I am divorcing you' and sign it, and it was legally binding. The wife had to leave, and find someone else to care for her, just had to leave. No rights. But now, women have more ability to leave the husband. Single parenting is becoming more and more common.

Some people think that dating shows objectify and sexualise women for entertainment. What do you think? How do you think it affects the women (and men) who watch it?

I think these shows are just for entertainment. And those women who chose to be on there, they are not really looking for a man from the show. Their idea is to make themselves famous across the world, so they will have more boys chase them. Men will know you initially, all men; this is their purpose. They ask stupid questions as a way for the public to remember. People may criticise this girl or that girl for being hungry for money, but you will remember her! She is getting her purpose fulfilled, she wants to be famous. My grandma is against these shows very much. Every time we watch this together, she asks why these women go on stage to be shown to men, like a commodity. People look at her and say 'I want her', like in a shop. She has this idea in her head. I really think this show is just for entertainment. The hosts always say that they match many couples, and make many people happy, but I think it is just to get attention.

When it comes to dating, what do you feel is important?

I have always had a feeling that a relationship and a marriage are two very separate things. For example, when searching for a relationship, the first thing to consider is the connection. Common interests, someone to talk to. You must share common topics. This is most important. I don't care if he is poor or rich, ugly or handsome (ok, maybe a little bit) but the most important bit is the feeling, the connection. But when it comes to marriage, other factors appear. The connection is still an important factor, but there are others. These include, for example, you have to know whether or not he has a good enough job or not to support a family. I don't really want my mother to support me, I want to be independent, but I don't want to earn more than my husband. You have to consider his job. And another is family. In China, marriage is not just the joining of two people, but of two families. Because his family is your family now. If he has a really big family, it may bring issues to my small family. This could be an issue with cross cultural relationships. You also have to consider his characteristics. Some boys are charming, but charming to everyone! You may enjoy his romantic side during the relationship, but when it comes to marriage you need to marry a man who is willing to commit. This is why I think marriage and relationships are two different things.

In a relationship, what is your role? Are you equal?

I expect an equal role in marriage. When I am searching for a boy or husband, I will want someone who can support me, and I can support him in return. Both financially and emotionally. He can talk to me about his problems, and I can talk to him about my problems. And also money; I expect good presents from him, but I too will buy good presents for him. Maybe expensive, I don't know. It is equal. I know some girls always expect their boyfriends to buy them something good or expensive, but if a boy did that for me I would do it back. An equal role is what I'm looking for. Cooking, cleaning, that can be shared. I am not good at cooking, so we can share that, ha ha! When I conjure images of my life in the future, I see him doing to cooking and me doing the cleaning… that would be a really good life for me. I expect an equal role, money wise and emotionally.

If you could sum up Chinese attitudes to these topics in a few sentences, what would they be?

I think that attitudes towards women and the status of women in Chinese society are getting more and more affected by the Western culture. It means women are getting more equally treated in society, but we still a long way to go. This is happening all over China. In some modern cities, like Shanghai or Beijing, or Shenzhen, things are better, you can easily find 'career women', women who are focussed on their job, but in the rural areas you can still find women who are not treated well. That is pretty sad. Chinese society is getting more and more affected by the Western culture, but some is still affected by traditional culture; they have these images in their heads of what Chinese women should do. But I think it is getting better and better. There are so many Chinese studying abroad now, and in ten years, they will become the mainstream in society, and they will have been greatly influenced by Western culture. So I think in a decade from now it will be even better. Women will be able to be more independent, more confident. With more opportunities, and treated better.

TIANJIN

August 2013, Southampton, UK.

Iris was born and raised in Tianjin, an ancient city near Beijing, in 1989. Since the age of seven she has lived with her paternal grandparents. She has been in the UK studying Fashion Design for almost a year, having studied in Portsmouth University before moving to Southampton University, and the University of Xi'an in Northern China before that. Her father works for a major German car manufacturer, whilst her mother stays at home. Her father travels very often for business, and is home just three or four days a month. They divorced over ten years ago.

Before my parents got divorced, they were always fighting and my father used to hit my mum. She was often rude to him, provoking him, and sometimes she defiled my father's mother. They always fought, all the time, and my mother always used to hit me when I was young... they used to try and get my to learn piano and painting and wei qing, *a traditional Chinese game. If I didn't want to go to piano class my mum would hit me, or slap me. My dad never hit me. That's why, after they divorced, I decided to stay with his parents. I was scared of her.*

Another strange thing... my father's mother, my nai nai, *didn't want my mother to marry my father because she is poor and uneducated, although my grandfather never had a problem with it. What is strange is that my grandmother is also poor and uneducated. She attacked my mother, saying she poor and stupid… so I think if you have a good education background you are more likely to think that love and happiness is more important than other things.*

How do you think future generations will view Chinese women in the early 21st Century?

For now, I think it depends… if a girl is from the city, it doesn't matter if she finds a good boy… it does matter though, I think. In cities, the parents will ask the girl to find a good boy. My paternal grandmother told my mother that she couldn't marry my father, as my father had graduated from Tianjin University, and my mother had only graduated from high school. I think the situation is still similar. If you don't have a good financial or educational background it is hard to find a good girl. I think that girls' thinking is more that they feel life isn't very good for them, and they want to find a boy as an easy way to become rich and have a better life. But for me, I think it doesn't matter as I have a kind of 'good' life; I don't want to find this type of boy, with too much money.

Many young Chinese women wear clothes that would not be accepted in previous generations. Are these clothes accepted now? If so, why?

I think that some people can't accept this style, this fashion. My aunty came to the UK last year and she travelled about, and I was wearing shorts, and she told me 'You can't wear that!' I asked why, and she replied that if I wore this style of clothes boys will think will I want to do something with them. But my classmates, they think it doesn't matter, so it depends. Young people they think is fine, but for people my aunt's age, around forty, they can't accept this. I think this is because China is now more open; we have absorbed some culture from the West that we can't understand. And we want to look nice; of course, every girl wants to look nice. We learn from dramas and programmes about different cultures, and that affects us.

What do you think has changed most since your mother was your age? Do you think anything should change further?

I don't know what has changed for my mum, during this time... we don't have too many conversations. But she did tell me she was very poor. She told me she had to ask her parents for permission to buy things, and often her parents couldn't afford what she wanted, and they'd get angry with her for asking for things they can't afford. That's why I try never to ask for things from my parents, they just give me things. I'm not spoilt, it's because they have just one child! This has changed. They want me to have a nice life, and they buy me lots of things. That's why so many Chinese study abroad now, because the parents want a good life for their child. Do you know Shanxi province? They are now rich due to huge coal deposits underground. Many people there can get very rich very quick there. Many children from there study abroad. Some people can earn a lot of money, and some people can't. It is just life.

Do women have equal opportunities and rights now?

I don't think women are treated equally yet. I remember, in high school, if I was to chat with a boy, the teacher would phone my parents and tell them I have a 'problem', but would do nothing to the boy. Is so unfair on me! They always said 'You can't do that, you can't change your hair colour, you can't wear make-up' but boys always get away with things. In some schools, where there is a female teacher, often they will fancy a boy, a student. That's true. And when they ask a question, and a girl answers wrong, the teacher will say something bad to the girl, discipline her. But if the boy gets it wrong, the teacher will say nothing. It's disgusting; I don't know what is wrong with Chinese teachers. And the salary [for women] is always lower than the man's. And in some trades they will say 'This job is just for men, not for women'.

In the UK and the US having a child out of wedlock is common. What do you think about this?

I think it is not good to have a child out of wedlock, as you can't feel stable with your partner. It means that your partner can leave you anytime they please. And it isn't good for the child either. I don't know about the situation in the UK, but in China, if you are not married and you have children, the child can't have a good school or attend a good university or find a good job. We have identity cards, and on it will be written whether your parents are married or not. It shows which family you belong to, you see? It means you can't get a good education or a good job. It does matter in China... My parents are divorced, but they were married when they had me. I have kept my father's name. I saw a story in China that in Beijing a woman needed a certificate to prove she lived there in order to have her child there. There are so many people there, it is so overcrowded, so they are strict on how many people can move there or live there. You must apply to the government to ask permission to have a child there.

Some people think that dating shows objectify and sexualise women for entertainment. What do you think? How do you think it affects the women (and men) who watch it?

Dating shows don't matter to me, but it acts as a kind of motivation for boys. All the boys who can get a good girl are always very rich and successful and the show tells boys that they must become rich and successful to get a good girl. I think sometimes it's ok... you know these shows are fake? Someone tells her 'Ok, your job should be this' but in real life her job is different. They make her more attractive by saying she is wealthy, but it is a lie.

When it comes to dating, what do you feel is important?

I think what a girl wants depends on her feelings. When I talk with a boy, and he is nice and funny and has a sense of responsibility, it is ok. If I find him attractive it is ok, but if I don't, if he is not a good person, I won't care how rich he is. Even if he is super handsome, if I have no feelings for him I won't continue dating him, it doesn't matter about looks or money.

In a relationship, what is your role? Are you equal?

In a relationship, I think you need to be good friends and share everything. I think I should be beautiful for him and look after him, but he should also do that for me, and look after me. It doesn't matter who earns more, it depends on your ability; if he can earn more than me, that's great, but if he can't, it's not a problem. I wouldn't be happy to stay at home and look after the baby and the house, as I wouldn't have my own life. I would always have to look after the baby and the house and my husband and I wouldn't have my own life. I wouldn't be able to have fun or go out with friends. If you have your own job, you can make your own friends and have fun.

If you could sum up Chinese attitudes to these topics in a few sentences, what would they be?

I think normal people, to sum up Chinese feelings, need dividing by age. For people who are forty up, they would think women should just stay at home and look after the baby and be a good wife. My father found a new girlfriend and he thinks that she shouldn't have work, because she is a lawyer and he always told me that she shouldn't have that job as she is so busy. He thinks if she has a job like that she would not have time to look after him or look after children. So that is how that age group would think. But the younger generations are more open to change. I think boys always try to think of many ways to make women happy. Because there are more boys than girls in China, it can be very difficult to find a wife now. You have to try to find a way to make them happy and then marry them. Otherwise the boy will stay single forever! They will do housework for their girls, and look after the baby for the girl. Almost a change in roles. If I had a boyfriend, even in high school, the boy would always look after me very, very well. Like when we have lunch he would always wait for me. I had a nice boyfriend in high school. I would always choose my favourite dish and he would wait for me, maybe forty minutes! He always walked me home and then walk back his own way alone.

ZHEJIANG

November, 2013. London, UK.

Janet was born in November 1989 in Zhejiang province. Her father and mother are both civil servants, both from Zhejiang. Janet has been in the UK one year one month at the time of interview. She studies Creative Industries and Art and Design in London as a Masters. She studied at the Chinese Academy of Arts in Hangzhou, Zhejiang province. This is her first time to leave China. She has travelled around the UK, including Scotland and Northern Ireland, Manchester and Liverpool. She enjoys her course, and enjoys drawing and designing. She also enjoys listening to and playing music, as well as horticulture, in her spare time.

How do you think future generations will view Chinese women in the early 21st Century?

Actually, my friends, some of those around me, all have happy lives. They can do what they want to do, because their parents want them to be happy. Many want to study abroad, so their parents pay for them to study in the UK or America. They can do what they want, learn to sing or dance or go to a famous university. Their parents try to create a good environment for them. They, like me, have happy lives and we are thankful for this. But I understand some girls who are not so rich… one of my roommates in China, her father died very early, and although her mother remarried, she needs to earn money for her brother to get married. Her mother can't afford it, so after she graduated she got a job to get money. I asked her 'Why do you need to get a job so early, and earn money early?' and she told me 'My brother needs it'. And he only has a high school education, he didn't go to university. But she needs to get money for him. I don't think that is very equal. But my other roommates are like me, not so bad. I think Chinese girls work harder than boys. That is what I think, but maybe this is not reality… but I know many girls work very hard to get a good job. I had twenty-five classmates in my university, and just five of them were boys. And these boys are not so smart. Because at the end of term we had to check our performance and the boys were never at the top, ha ha! And the girls have plans for after their studies; they want to get a Masters degree, and the boys don't seem to want to, they want to graduate and just get a job and earn money. So I think Chinese girls now are very ambitious and have their own plans, as they think that having a good husband is not the only way to change their lives. And it is hard for women in the working world. Many places do not like to employ women. At the job centre or employment agency you can see notices that say 'we only employ men'. Business jobs, things like that. Human resource departments prefer boys to girls, I don't know why. Maybe too many girls apply for these jobs, so it is easier for boys. Girls must work hard to out-do boys. Lots of pressure to be harder working than boys. In the Chinese work environment, they prefer boys to girls. But actually, I think boys are very smart.

They will not have to leave to have a baby or get married, they can commit easier. Girls have so many things, like having a baby and looking after the baby, which will interfere with work.

Many young Chinese women wear clothes that would not be accepted in previous generations. Are these clothes accepted now? If so, why?

It is accepted to wear sexier clothes now. Sometimes, when we play with our friends, like a meal or KTV, we can wear very sexy clothes. But sometimes I think a lot of Chinese will remind themselves not to wear very sexy clothes, if they see their parents or grandparents. Every day, when I saw my grandparents, my mother would not allow me to wear a short dress or any such things. My grandma always tells me 'You want to wear that short a dress? It is so cold! It is not good for your health!' but yes, I think it is accepted now. You see a lot of Chinese girls on the street wearing lots of makeup and sexy clothes. I think this is because people's minds change. Five years ago, people thought this style is flirtatious, suggestive, that you are not a good girl. And some people may think 'This girl is slutty and easy'. If I had a child, I would not want my child to play with that sort of girl. That she is a bad girl, a party girl. But now, because the fashion changes, people think it is ok.

What do you think has changed most since your mother was your age? Do you think anything should change further?

One day my mother told me she didn't need to go to university because back then the government could help the people who live in cities to find jobs; they planned jobs for them. They didn't need to worry. That period had less people in universities. The examinations were so hard. So my mum just waited for the government to offer her a job. At that time there was a policy which encouraged people, young people, to go to the countryside. This was cancelled under Deng Xiao Ping. My mother told me that my grandmother wanted her to go to the countryside to work. But my mother didn't go for some reason... but it was more common for girls to go to the countryside, because boys can work in the city. Because parents want their sons to work; their daughters were not so important.

Do women have equal opportunities and rights now?

Employers don't like women so much, they prefer men. And in the home, it is not about equality. All Chinese people think the man should be stronger than the woman. All the men must earn more than their wives, and make the decisions. They need to be strong, make the decisions, and the woman must obey. If the woman happens to be higher, have a higher social level (if her job is better than the husbands', or they earn more money, or work for the government), people consider it very strange. I think this type of family is strange. The man needs to be better than the woman. Wives can be strong though. Many things need her decision... actually, if we say that women should be equal, this sort of family may be normal [to British people], but to

215

Chinese it is strange. In education girls are treated the same… except ugly girls, ha ha! The teacher won't like them! But if a girl is a beauty and gets good grades, she will be favoured… but I think in university it is the same. I think boyfriends will always help their girlfriend to carry bags! But I think British people are so nice; when I went back to China, I had a heavy package and someone helped me on the London underground. It is very normal here, habitual. But in China, no. I think many girls in China would not expect help, from anyone. But in the street, beautiful girls are looked at by many men, and helped by many men. But only if they have a beautiful face, ha ha!

In the UK and the US having a child out of wedlock is common. What do you think about this?

If the girl's family is very wealthy, her child with take her name, rather than the father's. This is because her family is better connected or owns a business. They would need an heir the most, to carry on the family business, to inherit their stuff. I think having a baby out of wedlock is not a good thing; it depends on our parents. If our parents disallow us to have a child out of wedlock… and some people in society would judge us, and think we are bad girls. And if I had a baby together with a man but without being married, what would happen if he decided to leave? The baby would not have a father. That would not be good at all. If the boy really wants to love the baby and take care of the child, then it doesn't matter if you are married or not. It is just about responsibility.

Some people think that dating shows objectify and sexualise women for entertainment. What do you think? How do you think it affects the women (and men) who watch it?

I think that women have the right to make themselves look beautiful, but I don't think dating shows are a good guide for women. Because women on these shows just show themselves in order to become topics of conversation. This show can make them famous and attract attention. I know these shows require interviews, and you will be monitored on your performance and communication before you go on the show. And they direct your questions. Like the girl that said 'I would rather cry in a BMW than laugh on a bicycle'... I'm not one to judge, but I don't like that. Some girls, I think maybe they have fake stories; they lie. They are just twenty-one or twenty-two, but they claim to have MA levels. I am twenty-four and I am still studying for my MA, I have only just graduated my undergraduate. They are trying to show 'I am a perfect woman, you need to choose me'. Boys often tell me that if they like a girl, they like her. They don't mind if she wears makeup or not, they don't want her to change for them. Because they really like her, the way she is. Original, ha ha! I think this show is so bad, as this sentence about BMWs and bicycles has become a slogan for Chinese women. Do you know *fen qing*, young people who rebel against things they think are wrong, against social wrongs? Well, many girls feel like becoming *fen qing* over this. Many Chinese girls don't like her because of this. But she has become famous! But I think, on the other side, there are some Chinese girls who like money, and this is their reality. It depends on different areas; some parts in the east, like Zhejiang, Shanghai, Fujian, are more open to wisdom. We can judge what is right or not. But some girls from the middle of the mainland, these provinces, a lot of them just chase money. Do you know *bao fa hu*? *Bao fa hu* means like... the Great Gatsby. Become very rich in one night. Some in the middle of mainland China dug a hole and found oil and just became very rich in a couple of years. But they don't think education is very important, or skills are very important, they just rely on these resources and get rich quick. My mother told me we don't need to judge them, and that they are simply very lucky to get this money. It is always a way to chase your dreams.

When it comes to dating, what do you feel is important?

I think communication is most important. Mentally, morally, we are compatible. And from that I can know what he thinks about problems and society. He needs to have a nice face; not handsome, just nice is ok. So when you see him first time you think he is very kind, not a bad man, a convict... a kind face. I think *guanxi* depends. It cannot be said that this is very important, but if he had a very good connection it is a very good resource for us. But if he didn't have this, it is ok. Because I think a good boy, a clever boy, with a good education, will have a good capability to create his own connections. If he can create his own, it doesn't matter if he currently has them or not. He would have to be local to me too. To me, I think foreigners are ok, but it's better to be Chinese because our parents and grandparents would prefer a Chinese boy because of the language barrier and cultural differences. It would be better to have a Chinese, but I think many Chinese girls now like foreign boys. Because foreign boys are very funny! They are very open.

In a relationship, what is your role? Are you equal?

I like cooking, so I would cook for him, it doesn't matter if I *must* or *should*. And I don't think I would like being 'eye candy', he [her boyfriend] said he doesn't want me to work too hard, he doesn't care about that. Maybe I would go back to China and get a teaching job, not so much pressure, and with several holidays. But never a housewife! My boyfriend thinks I should have my own life and career, not just look after a baby or the house my whole life. If there is housecleaning or something, we both work together to do it. I think this will be the life of Chinese girls in the future. Because very beautiful people are just a small group, the rest just use their skills to earn money rather than just our faces. Sometimes I think men work very hard, so women have their own responsibilities to clean and help him.

If you could sum up Chinese attitudes to these topics in a few sentences, what would they be?

I don't think all Chinese women would agree with my opinion… *bai jin nu* girls… money diggers I think in English, gold diggers. They simply cannot understand our ideas of New Women in this new generation. Sometimes we define ourselves as this. But most of my friends agree with me, and have similar values to mine. And people in different areas, like the east and west. Those in the east cannot recognise this, they cannot understand we need to be new women, they are happy as they are. We always recognise problems in China. Not many Chinese can study in Europe or America, we are not a huge group. We had twenty-five in our class in China, and only two or three went abroad. Maybe I think I am right, and we share similar values, but we are all different. This is reality, we cannot fight it.

Printed in Great Britain
by Amazon